Blood Wet Rose

Dr. Dane

Summary

In the very last installment of THE MIDNIGHT ROSE series, be a part of Sam and her own circle of relatives over again as they address love, ache and anguish. Who will live to tell the tale this time? Who may be hurt? Will she get her happiy ever after or will she move down with the ship? Join your favorite characters. In eel-e book order: 1: The Midnight Rose 2: Shattered Rose 3: Academy of the Rose 4: Blood Soaked Rose Don't neglect about to like, remark and review!

Chapter One

I became pacing backward and forward in my room as Cody took a nap, Brian looking my each pass as he knew I became flustered. "How is it that that is even possible! Hayden stated he showed her death! She slit her wrists in a bathtub!

She can't be **right here!**" I whisper shout. "I haven't any concept Samantha, however I don't like it. They so **show up** to get on a flight with you, you **have been** on my own with Cody and that they simply stroll beyond you want it's nothing. They **need to** be **making plans** some thing. Why **could** Lezzy **also be** with Craig, he's a nobody" Brian grumbles, his **arms** rubbing over his face with stress. "I'm calling Jayden and getting him **to** return back get Cody, I **want** him as **a long way** far far from her as possible. Beck's entering into touch with Hayden to discern him out and I **haven't any concept** what **they'reas much as!**" I improve my **arms** in exasperation. "So you're staying **right here?**" Brian asks. "Until I **discover** what **they're** doing, yes. Jayden and the others will **guard** the kids, **however** I can't have them **close** to her. Not after **remaining** time." I say as I **appearance** over my little boy, **drowsing** like an angel. "No one is ever going **to the touch** him **once more** Sammy, you don't **want to fear approximately** that" Brian smiles, his hand taking mine. My telecell smart phone earrings as I quick solution earlier **than** it wakes Cody. "Hey babe" I solution. "Hey, what's going on? Harvey **stated** it became an emergency" Jayden stated in a panic. "I want you to return back and get Cody, take him domestic and live a long way from right here." I solution. "Why?" He asks. "Lizzy, she's now no longer dead...She's right here...with Craig, I don't recognize what they' regambling at, however they have been on my plane. I don't need our boy every where close to them whilst I discern this out, so I want to recognize he's secure. Promise me, you'll get him and preserve him secure." I say as Brian squeezes my hand in support. "You recognize I could die for him Sammy. I'll get a flight as quickly as I can. We'll cope with this Kitten. I'll take hold of one of the men to include me. Any options from the little man?" Jayden replies. "Taylor or Grandpa, he loves them each" I solution. "Done. We'll discern this out. Stay secure, I'll be there as quickly as I can" "Love you Jay" I smile. "Love you too Kitten" He says as he hangs up. "You are sickening" Brian faux gags and I laugh. "You're simply jealous" I smirk shoving him playfully. "Shut up" He groans and receives up. "Where are you going?" I ask. "I'm going to look if Beck's discovered some thing out" He says as I nod. Jayden: Taylor's coming with me, we've a flight in hours.

Hold on baby, we're coming xx Sammy: See you quickly, be careful. Tell Taylor to go to my antique house, he is aware of the manner xx Jayden: Your antique house? The one which burnt down. X Sammy: They rebuilt it. It's lovely Jay, I can't wait a good way to see it x Jayden: See you quickly, I love you each. Tell Brian he higher preserve my lady and little boy secure xx Sammy: Just get right here, I'm able tore taining us secure babe. Brian's simply an advantage gun x Jayden: Oh I recognize you could cope with yourself, however you don't want to do it on my own x Sammy: I recognize. Just get your ass right here. See you quickly xx Jayden: Love you, see you quickly Kitten x "Mummm" Cody mumbles as he wakes up from his nap as I smile and select out him up. "Have a terrific nap kiddo?" I ask as he clings to me. "Still sleepy Mummy" he mumbles as I chuckle. "Daddy's coming right here today" I say as he perks up. "DADDY!" He squeals in my ear. "You're going to headdomestic with him. I want to type out a fewdullpaintings and I can't watch you all of the time, so he's bringing Uncle Taylor right here with him to get you after which you'll cross domestic whilst I type it out after which I'll come domestic to you. Is that ok?" I inform him as he frowns. "Mummy live whilst Cody cross domestic?" He frowns. "Yes, however mummy will come domestic quickly" I reply. "No. Mummy come domestic now with Cody" He huffs. "Cody, I can't, I actually have paintings to do" I sigh. "Cody need Mummy to return back domestic!" Cody screams. "Woah there, buddy! What's with the screaming?" Brian is available in quickto look Cody grumpy in my fingers. "Mummy no come domestic with Cody." "Cody, I want mummy to assist me with a few paintings. But it's now no longer some thing you could be right here for. We'll be very busy. I will deliver Mummy domestic cwhilst we're done. I will come together along with her for a go to too yeah?" He says as I see Cody ponder in his head. "Uncle Brian include Mummy domestic?" Cody mumbles. "Yes, I'll come domestic with mummy" He smiles and takes Cody's hand. "Fine, Cody crossdomestic with Daddy and Uncle Tay, however Mummy come later wit Uncle Bwian." Cody nods as I sigh in comfort kissing his head and nodding to Brian in thanks. "How approximately we visit the park?" Brian smiles as Cody's face lighting up with pleasure as he scrambles out of my fingers and runs into Brian's as they run off downstairs. I observe a bit behind, grabbing my gun and hiding it in a holster below my jacket, simply in case. "Make certain you positioned a coat on him!" I shout down the stairs. "Yes MUM" Brian laughs, and I shake my head with a smirk. We get prepared to visit the park and slowly stroll there it wasn't a long way at all. "Mummy antique park?" Cody faces me and factors. "Yeah buddy, my mummy used to deliver me right here too" I smile. I recollect me and Jason gambling on this park thankfully earlier than our complete lives modified for the worse. "Mummy sad..." He frowns and stops. "Mummy simply misses her mummy" Brian ruffles Cody's appropriate curly, mouse brown hair. "Mummy come play with Cody" Cody grabs my hand and drags me with him to the swings. I location him with inside the swing as he giggles after I push him, screaming to head better as Brian takes some pictures people all collectively. Brian takes Cody to the sand pit as I watch them collectively from the bench. "He seems healthy" the bench creaks as a person joins me at the bench as I flinch. "You shouldn't be right here" I growl.

"Sam, please, I'm now no longer going to harm him. I'm sorry" Lizzy says as I study her. "Leave. I don't need you close to my son" I snap. "Ok. But we want your assist" Lizzy sighs status as I note Brian get up, alert with Cody in his fingers. "Why must I assist you? You faked your personal death...You attempted to kill my son...Why must I assist you?" I ask as I sign for Brian to head domestic. "Mummy!" Cody screams for me as Brian walks off. "Mummy might be there quickly baby!" I shout as he cries in Brian's fingers, kicking and screaming. "I won't harm him" Lizzy says. "That's what I concept remaining time...Look what befell then..." I growl. "Just promise you'll assist me, and I will by no means ask some thing of you once more. I won't cross close to Cody" "What do you want me for?" I ask, my eyes scouring the area. "Craig heard approximately a person going up towards my father. He absolutely sponsored Bryant however has controlled to preserve quiet these kinds of years. No one is aware of who he is. Until Craig heard some matters in prison...He has some buddies interioner none the less listening for him. This guy desires to take down each mafia known. He desires overall lmanage and the Midnight Rose is one of the ones he desires. My father and you'vea number ofthe largest mafia corporations with inside the world. This guy threatens the complete stability you need to preserve. I pretended to die to head below the radar. Turns out this man likes younger blondes, he's into the entirety we hate. Human trafficking, inter course earrings, all of it. I want your assist to take him down or we should all die" She says as I appearance in her eyes, looking for whether or not she became telling the truth. "Why must I believe both you or Craig?" I ask. "You cherished me once...I owe you a large debt after what I did. But I will now no longer have my father killed. He's attempted to assist me so often as I've failed him time and time once more. Just as I failed you. Craig became in my clinic...We talked he's been supporting me..." She says as I laugh. "He's supporting you...This is Craig...He loves to play with women, pulled a gun on me and my Grandpa...He doesn't assistall and sundryhowever himself" I say snidely. "Just take this. It has the entire tywe've so a long way. My new variety is in there. No depend what though, Cody is secure from me. I'm higher, I swear. I've been taking my medicinal drugs and Craig talks to me. I'm higher I swear" She says delivering an envelope. "I'll study it. No promises. I'll be in touch" I say as I start to stroll away. "Thank you Sammy" She sighs. "Just recognize Lizzy, you go me or my own circle of relatives this time, there's a bullet together along with your call on it" I growl as she nods and walks away. "Sammy! You're ok!" Beck drives as much as me at the mannerre turned with more than one his guys with inside the vehicle as they get out, searching across the area, looking for Lizzy. "She's gone" I say, and that they nod at me. "Get with inside the vehicle" Beck orders as I get in and we force some seconds down the street to the house. Getting out as I race into the house, listening to Cody screaming out. "Baby, mummy's right here, I'm right here" I say as I kneel in the front of him as his tears soak my t-shirt. "What befell?" Brian asks. I throw the envelope onto the desk as he simply seems at it. Beck's the primary to seize it and open it. "I'd heard rumours approximately this...I didn't assume it became true..." Beck stated. "Sammy!" Jayden's voice shouted from the door as they knocked heavily. "Daddy!" Cody squeals as I take hold of him and race to the door establishing it. "Hey there buddy" Jayden smiles as Cody jumps from my fingers and into his. "Why are you wearing, we've a trouble face?" Taylor asks as they input the house. "Daddy, uncle bwian take me from park whilst mummy speak to lady!" Cody grumbles angrily. "What lady?" Taylor increases a brow. "Lizzy" I solution, and he stands nonetheless in shock. "She's imagined to be dead..." He says. "Yeah, that's what all of usconcept. But, believe me, she's alive" I sigh as we take a seat down withinside theliving room as Cody hugs into Jayden tightly. "You want to study this Sam" Beck arms the envelope to me as I take out the papers interior, Taylor searching over my shoulder. I checked outa number of the images. "Hold on, that's one in all your Grandpa Jon's gala's from years ago...Look, that's you" Taylor factors to me with inside the image, I became approximately fifteen with inside the image. "This one too... But that's the boarding faculty dance...This guy, he became our head master...Why is he in all of those images?" I ask trying to Beck. "Look at the opposite page" He says as I deliver out any other, it describes, people, places, places of intercourse trafficking earrings. Then the call of the pinnacle of the Mafia... "No mannerbecame Mr Henderson the chief of any other mafia" Taylor gasps. "Hold on, the headmaster of your antique boarding faculty is the chief of a few mafia? What do Lizzy and Craig need to do with this?" Jayden asks. "Daddy what's a ma...mafa...mafia?" Cody asks as I tilt my head returned and groan. "Oh, uhh, it's a totally massiveown circle of relatives that protects people. But a few aren't so nice." Jayden solutions and he appears to simply take it and retain gambling. "This is why Lizzy desires me... I can get near them with out suspicion, they already recognize me. But they don't recognize that I recognize approximately them" I say. "You're now no longer doing it on my own" Taylor says. "You need to cross domestic with Cody and Jayden" I urge. "No, Brian can go together with them. We went to that faculty collectively. They recognize we stick collectively like glue. We try this collectively. Like antique times" Taylor says. "I don't recognize..." I sigh. "He's right. You each knew this guy earlier than. You should get in the direction of him." Beck says. "Looks like we're going returned to faculty" I groan.

Chapter Two

"Mummy come domesticquickly" Cody sniffles as I hug him tight on the airport. "Mummy can bedomestic as quickly as she can. Love you infant boy" I kiss his head and cuddle him tightly. "I'll appearance after mummy Cody" Taylor smiles and ruffles his hair as he giggles and smacks his hand away. I by skip Cody to Brian as Jayden comes as much as me and wraps his palms round my waist. "You higher come domestic in a single piece, kitten" he whispers into my ear so Cody can't hear. "I will do my high-quality. I will usually do my high-quality to get domestic to my family. I'm going to overlook you men" I kiss him passionately at the lips as his fingers thread into my hair. "You higher come domestic, we've got plans in your birthday" Jayden smiles pecking my lips as Brian gags at the back of us, Cody giggling. "I'll do my high-quality" I smile. "Look after my female Taylor" Jayden bro hugs Taylor. "I usually have" He solutions with a smirk. I visit hug Brian and Cody collectively as Cody laughs on theinstitution hug. "Love you infant boy, you too pungent Uncle Brian" I smirk. "Take care Sam, we'll see you quickly" Brian nods at Beck and Taylor. "I love you" Jayden kisses me a very last time earlier than taking Cody in his palms. "I love you all" I say, maintainingreturned the tears. "Bye mummy!" Cody waves as they head off closer to the jet. "Bye infant! Take care of daddy!" I shout as they flip the corner. "They'll be ok" Taylor locations a hand on my shoulder because the tears escape. "I recognize they will" I sigh as he is taking my hand and we exit to the automobile that waited for us. "I known as Henderson this morning" Taylor says riding to the residence. "You what?!" I exclaim searching at him like he became crazy. "You recognize I became his favorite man or woman returned in school. So, I known as him, informed him we have been return don the town for some time and whether or not we'd be capable of visit...Turns out he's walking a gala for capacitytraders to the school. He's invited us with open palms" He smirks. "You intricate little devil" I smirk. "Now, we ought toparent out what to do with Lizzy and Craig" He sighs as we pull into the force. "Unfortunately, I assume we'll ought toconsist of them. They recognizeextra than we do. Plus, he's after each families. Hayden nevertheless doesn't have a clue approximately any of this. I talked to her this morning and she or he doesn't need him to discovertill we're accomplished with this or he'll pull her out. I ought toconsider her, she's controlled to get a variety ofrecordsapproximately this man that we didn't even recognizeapproximately. We get this accomplished, we take him down after which she is goingreturned to her father." I say. "You neverthelesssense for her don't you" Taylor sighs. "I hate and love her on theequal time. She almost ruined my existence taking my baby from me, however she's been destroyed with the aid of using our manner of existence. What if I had long past down the equalroute as her? I've been destroyed with the aid of usingguys too. It might have been me" "That's whereinyou're strong. You take some thing and need to make it higher. You need to resolve issues, love all and make a higher world. You are the foundationfor thus many. Now, we're going to get via this, you'll movedomesticon yourchild and lover, I will movedomestic to my husband and Lizzy can move on her merry manner and do anything she does. Just don't allow them to distract you" Taylor says, and I nod. "I won't allow them to distract me. We get in, verify our records, take him out, wreck his mafia and movedomestic. Threat long past." I state. "All earlier than your birthday marvel" Taylor smirks and I spherical to him. "Surprise? Tell me Taylor!" I smile playfully. "No! You won't make me talk!" Taylor laughs as he rushes into the residence. "Taylor! Tell me!" I chase after him as he laughs, jumping over the eatingdesk with a laugh. "No manner. They will kill me for telling you" "But..." I flutter my eyelashes. "No! I'm now no longer telling you, don't flutter them at me, it doesn't work" He laughs. "Fine. Keep your grimy secrets" I groan. "Get your shit collectively Sammy. We are going to the cabin" He smiles as I squeal. My domesticfarfar fromdomestic, our antique cabin we had whilst we moved out of the school. "You're joking right? I idea you bought it" I exclaim. "Nah, I've been renting it out. We simply had a vacancy, so I idea why now no longermove there for a toucheven as." "Great!" I smile as we accumulate up a number of our gear. "Sammy here" I solution my telecellsmartphonebecause itearrings loudly in my pocket. "It's Beck. We've had phrase from Lizzy that she's already on direction to the school. She and Craig can be posing as capacitytraders, as will I. We will all mingle with others and maintain Henderson in view in any respect times. You'll be capable of get the nearest to him aleven though so be careful. We are sufferingto attach him to whatever, Craig's records isn't in our reach, I don't accept as true with him. So maintain your head to the ground, listen, play your elementproperly with Lizzy and Craig, there can beextra to this than they may be letting on" Beck says. "Do you watched there's a opportunity he's now no longerthe top of a mafia?" I ask as Taylor eyes me. "I'm now no longer sure. Everything I've dug up indicates he's as a minimuma part of one, however I can't discoverwhatever on him being a fewkind of leader. But if Lizzy is right, he's storedproperly-hidden for a protracted time. It will be true, however I'm nevertheless unsure" Beck solutions. "He becamebuddies with my Grandfather, it wouldn't marvel me in the event that theyhave been in all of itcollectively" I say as I positioned my rucksack on my returned. "Just, be careful. Just remember, we don't recognizeeverydifferenton the gala" Beck says. "Sorry, who're you?" I smirk. "Good female. Do get your selfa pleasingget dressedeven as you're at it. It's a flowery gala, get dressed as you will have in your grandfather. Henderson will anticipate it. You'll ought tofaux to be unswerving to the reminiscence of him. It's your high-quality option" "Yeah, I idea that. I'm on it. Stay secure Beck. See you on the gala" I say and grasp up. "He doesn't assume Lizzy is telling the entiretale does he?" Taylor says and I sigh and shake my head. "We can't be positivealeven though. We get in and discover. If she is telling the fact then our mafia's are in grave danger. If she's lying, we'll discover" I say as we head out of the residenceand cargo Brian's car. "It's bizarre being returneddomestic..." Taylor sighs searchingon theresidence. "I recognize, it will likely be even more bizarreon the cabin and the school" I nod as we head off closer to our antique cabin. Damien: We pass over you men already! Stay secure *Photo of Damien and Cody gamblingat the ground* xx "Aww, Damien simplydespatched me a text. He despatched an photo of him and Cody at thegroundgamblingtogether along with his blocks" I smile as Taylor in briefappears over with a smile. "He'd make a notable dad right?" Taylor smiles. "Oh yeah, you each would" I smile. "We have beenconsidering adopting one of theyoungsterson the school" Taylor says. "Really! That's first rate Taylor!" I exclaim happily. "Thanks Sammy, it methodplentywhich youaid us so much" "I usually will Taylor, you're my high-qualitypal, you've been there nearly my entireexistence. We aideverydifferent. I don't recognizewherein I'd be with out you. You're one of themotives I haven't come to be like Lizzy. You assistrestore me each time I'm damaged and shattered, You're the glue in my heart" I smile putting a hand on his thigh. "Best buddiesfor all time right?" He smiles squeezing my hand in his. "Forever" I smile as we placed ona fewsong for the force ahead. It becamefirst rate having this experience with him like antique times. I ignored having my high-qualitypal to myself, we'd usually been there for everydifferent and the arena had driven us asidea touch. Now we ought to get a whilecollectively, solvingevery other piece of our world.

Chapter Three

"Sam! Get the fuck out of mattress!" Taylor shouts at me day after today as I'm curled up in my vintagemattress. I awaken smirking. This become familiar, we'd woken this manner many times, his shouting at me to get up. "I'm up!" I shout returned with a chuckle. "We wantto head get ourselves more than oneclothes for the gala the following daynight time. It's a masquerade party" He says as I sigh. "That makes it a touchgreater difficult" "I realize. We'll manage" He nods as I get up, washed and preparedto head out. "Where do you suspect you're going? What befell to our morning run?" He smirks as I get outdoorprepared for shopping. "You aren't serious?" I chuckle. "We're returneddomestic, of direction I'm serious. I overlooked this area. Don't you needto head on our trail? Don't you pass over it?" He smiles as I rush returned in and get into a couple of leggings and sports activities bra. "Let's passsluggish coach" I say as I jog immediatelybeyond him onto the forest trail. "You're off form Sammy! Not sufficienteducation after Cody" He smirks racing beyond me as I push thru the ache of my muscular tissues burning. It become true, I had overpassedhealth as I targetedat thefaculty and Cody. I needed to get returned to my heighthealth. I mightbegineducationonce moreafter Iwere givendomestic. "I...had...a...baby" I pant as we get returned to the the front door. "That become over a 12 months ago" Taylor laughs throwing me a bottle of water. "Shut up" I growl as he simply laughs. "Go batheafter which we'll passdiscover aget dressed for you and a smashing healthy for me" He smiles as I head upstairs, knackered already. "That is the one!" Taylor exclaims as he seems at me withinside thepurple and black corseted get dressed. "Do you suspect?" I smile, I cherished it and was hoping it wouldn't get ruined on the gala, it become too quite, the get dressed went to my ankles, some ruffles withinside the skirt giving it formbecause the corset held in my belly and made my cleavage appearance huge. "I should take a image for Jayden, he'll be wanking to that every one12 months" Taylor laughed getting his telecellsmartphone out as I posed some times, giggling. He despatched the message and as I become getting modifiedyet again I heard him gigglingtoughoutdoor. "What?" I asked. "Your guymight also additionally have simply exploded!" Taylor laughs as I pay attention my telecellsmartphone. "Hey baby" I say seductively. "You want to get that quite little ass of yours domestic kitten" He growls lustfully. "I will, after I'm accomplished, perhaps I'll convey the get dresseddomestic too" "You appearance fucking horny. I don't like that human beings are going to be looking you in it" Jayden says. "But there may be one aspect" I say. "What?" He growls. "I'm now no longer theirs. I'm yours. They don't get to contact, bear in mind that." I whisper to him. "God rattling it kitten" He moans. "How's my baby?" I ask converting the concern as he groans at me, I chuckle. "He's fine, lacking his mum, however we've were given him distracted. Cody has Grandpa wrapped round his little finger. Harvey has been on Cody responsibility for a even as. I nearlyby no means get him" Jayden answers. "Good, I pass over you men too. But with a bit of luck we'll be accomplishedquickly. The gala is the following day, we'll get this accomplishedand are availabledomestic" I say. "Just be cautious Kitten. I shouldpass our son desires tovisit the park. Love you my horny kitten" He says. "I love you too, inform Cody mummy loves him" I say earlier than we grasp up. "You good enough in there?" Taylor peeks in. "Fine..." I sniff, a tear falling from my cheek. "We'll be domesticquickly, and you may get returnedin your boys" He smiles. Taylor choices a cleverhealthy that suits him flawlessly as he chooses a tie which suits the purple of my get dressed. "Looking precise buddy" I say searching at my first-classbuddyattempting out the healthy. "I do tidy up properly don't I?" He smirks as I take a image of him and ship it to Damien as he calls Taylor as Jayden had me. "I realizeyou want it baby...I'll be domesticquicklysufficient...But I like it, you may't tear it...But...Fine you may rip it off me" Taylor groans as I chuckletough. "If you are prettycompleted having amusing..." A deep voice sounds at the back of me as Taylor says good-byequick and I flipto stand Craig and Lizzy. "What are you doing right here?" I ask. "We want to get dressed up too. But we're taking this seriously, in contrast toa number of us" Craig growls as I take a breakthrough to him. "Enough, equal team" Lizzy steps withinside thecenterpeople. "Are we?" I increase a brow. "Of directionwe're" She frowns. "I wish so. Now do you thoughts, we're leaving, exceptyou've got gota few new records?" I add. "Nothing new. But right here, we had com hyperlinks made" She passes me what gave the look of an earring that stillheld on the pinnacle of my ear too, hiding the piece inside. "The rose on it's fara pleasantcontact don't you suspect?" Craig smirks. "My fist on your face could bea pleasantcontactin case you aren't cautious" I stated, however hated to admit, the roses that have been crawling round my ear have beena pleasantcontact. "You don't suppose it makes it apparent that she is aware ofapproximately the Midnight Rose?"

Taylor eyes it carefully. "By the seems of all of thepictures from preceding galas she constantly had roses on her somewhere, it'llappear to be she is reminiscing the coolest days" Lizzy stated. "She's proper" I nod. "Good, now go away, if we get noticedcollectively then we may be in trouble. Lizzy could becarrying an ear piece just like yours and Taylor, I had a small ear piece made for you. Should be small sufficient that no person will see it" He fingers it over and Taylor nods. "We've despatcheda few over to Beck too" Lizzy says. "Great. You higher be properapproximately all this" I say as I choose up my luggage with the get dressed. "You don't believe us?" Craig increases a brow. "I'd by no meansbelieve you. Lizzy is a one-of-a-kindaspect entirely" I growl. "You neverthelessbelieve me?" Lizzy says faintly. "I need to have the ability to" I sigh as we go away the store. "Movie night time like vintage times? Before the shit starts?" Taylor says with a understanding smile whilst we get to the car. "Sounds bestproper now" I smile. For the relaxation of the night time we pigged out on snacks even aslookingmovies like we used to. It becomea lotamusing as we messed round as we had earlier than, I hadn't laughed like that duringthis type oflengthy time. Soon sufficient it become time to visitmattress, however neither peopledesired to sleep alone. So we each slept in his mattress as we used to, hugging everydifferent. "Are you preparedto head Sammy?" Taylor asks as we end up our breakfast. Today become the day of the gala bur first Mr Henderson desired us to peer the facultyand are available see him. He desired to seize up with us earlier than the gala. We might get preparedon thefaculty. "As prepared as I can be" I smile and clutch my stuff even as we head off toward the faculty. "This feels so odd. I by no meansidea we'd come returnedright here" Taylor says as we head up the lengthy winding street to the faculty, noticing its grandeur. It had gotten largerconsidering the fact that we had left howeverneverthelessregarded so regal. "This area haunts my nightmares" I shiver. "I marvel what befell to the men who used to overcome on me earlier than you grew to become up like an avalanche and flattened them?" Taylor stated and I needed tochuckle. "One have become a instructorright here and the alternativehave become the waste of areas I stated they might. Fucked up, drugged up and 1/2 ofuseless zombies" I stated, I'd already checked, I become curious. "You stalker!" Taylor laughed as we parked. "I become curious!" I laughed as I shoved him playfully. Out of the nook of my eye I observed Mr Henderson popping out of the the front door with a tremendous smile on his face. "Here he comes" I say as Taylor turns and we placed on our façade. "Mr Henderson!" Taylor says with outstretched palms as they hug hello. "Well have a take a observe you each! So grown up! I wish I won't have to interrupt up any fights with you Samantha?" He smirks at me as he offers me a quick hug, searching me over. "No concerns there. I best punch if it's deserved" I wink as he chuckles. "Well! Come in! It's super to have you evereachright hereright now of 12 months. It will appearancesuper that a number of our precedingcollege studentsaid us. I even havea fewas an alternativemassivebuyers coming tonight. I'd such as youeachto satisfy them" He says as I eye Taylor. "Oh really? Why's that?" I ask. "They've heard that the grand-daughter of Jon Jones could be there. They are intrigued which you didn't fall in his footsteps…You left domestic and by no means took over the commercial enterprise" He says. "It wasn't my aspect. I watched his commercial enterprisesmash him, piece through piece till he died" I sigh, pretending to overlook my grand-father. "It is a disgrace he died of this type ofunexpectedcoronary heart attack. He becomea person of…effective will" He says as he eyes me. He leads us to his workplace and gestures the chairs in the front of his desk. "I experience like a naughty facultywomanonce more" I chuckle sitting on the desk. "Have you been behaving Miss Jones? I don't doubt which you have prettythe desire to motive havoc as you probably didon your grandfather" He says beginning a draw and bringing out a folder as I eye it. "What's that?" Taylor asks as Mr Henderson places a finger to his lips. "Just your vintagedocuments, I ideayou may do with having a laugh at your vintage escapades." He says as I open it. Photos of me, Taylor, the lads, Grandpa, Lizzy… Then greaterrecords on Hayden, Lizzy and Craig. They have been all in a imagecollectivelyoutdoor of the jail Craig wereinstalled as I have a take a observe Mr Henderson huge eyed. He starts writing on a be aware pad as he startsto speak playfully approximately our vintagemethods at schools. They aren't who you suspect they are. I am NOT your enemy. I even haveattempted to shield you out of your grandfather for years till you subsequently did some thing I shouldnow no longer. You were given out of his fingers. I mightby no meansharm you Samantha. My eyes scour the web pageafter whichappearance to his face as he brings out every other envelope. Inside are letters upon letters from my grandfather, Jon. I knew his hand writing, they have been his alright. Taylor and Mr Henderson carried on speakme as I examinethru them. My grandfather and Mr Henderson argued in most, they argued approximately my future. Mr Henderson desired a one-of-a-kindexistence for me, my grandfather looking me beneathneath his wing...My grandfather had won. I'm being watched. Hayden isn't all he seems. He's dangerous. He'll be there tonight. He become your grandfather's buddy. Do NOT believe him or Lizzy. I nod as Taylor takes his flipanalyzing the office work in the front of me. I become confused, why the hell might Lizzy pass after Mr Henderson.

Could we believe him? I get out my telecellsmartphone and open the app that Damien had made that allows you tolocate any insectsthat might be withinside the room as I joked approximately beating the ladswithinside the cafeteria. The bookcase, a small recording tool as I pointed to it, Taylor nodding as he regarded it over. I persisted to scour the room howeverthere has been no differenttool. "Kill it" I mouthed as Taylor nodded and destroyed the bug. "We won't have lengthytill they word its gone. Why did you need to shield Sammy?" Taylor rounded to Mr Henderson. "I did it on yourmom. She and I have beenprecise friends, I promised I mightshield you with my existence" He answered. "That didn't paintings did it?" I snap. "I did my first-class I'm walking a facultyright here too. There becomebesta lot I should do! I went to each gala and persuaded human beingsnow no longerto shop for you. You don't have anyconceptwhat number ofhuman beingsdesired to smash you. It's take years for me to grow to be as effective as I even have! I don't needto peer you harmed howeverthere has beennot anything I should do. Hayden is aware of my moves!" He argued. "Why might Hayden needto headtowards me whilst he says he's my finestbest friend" I ask. "He desired your mom and misplaced to Gregory. So he set his eye on you. However, he wasn't so fortunate with that either. You escaped his clutches once more and once more. Without even realising it. Vern becomeone in all his minions and shortly Gregory have become an best friend to him in conjunction with your uncle. I don't realize what he's gambling at now, however I suppose he's the use of his personal daughter to get to you. He wishes me uselessdue to the fact he is aware of I realize the truth. He desires tosmashthe whole lot you've built. He's now no longerthe personyou suspecthe's Samantha" He says. "So, what will we do tonight?" Taylor ask, pacing the room. "We convey on. We fakewe'renevertheless with them. We'll locate Hayden and take him down. I'll inform Beck to put together for it. But I will make certain he best tells criticalhuman beings, simply in case we've gothuman beings in our ranks that aren't with us truly." I sigh. A knock at the door booms withinside the room as I take the envelopes and stuff them in my rucksack as Mr Henderson brings out a brand new folder, our actualdocuments as I chuckle at them. "Come in" He calls out with a nod at us. "Sir...we've got a...situation" The guy says searching at us earlier than realisation reaches his face. "Well, if it isn't Tony. Still bullying kids?" I ask with a smirk as he frowns. "No. I educateright here. Some peopledevelop up Samantha" He growls. "I can simplybelieve your lessons...You should be the PE instructor you have beenby no meansclever so it can't be something else" I chuckle. "No, I'm the English instructor" He grumbles as I burst into laughter. "English...seriously...You employed him for English...He failed 5 times!" I chuckle as I see the anger in his face as he stomps aheadhoweverword his eyes flicker to the bookcase. Oh so this manbecomea part of it...Go figure... "Now, now Samantha, do behave. You are right here as a visitor and I won't have you everpreventing in my faculty" Mr Henderson says sternly. "Sorry sir, I simply hate whilst little sneaks, slither approximately like they personal the area" I flip and flick my eyes over to the bookcase, hoping he'd understand. "Well, it'dappearwhich youwanta whilecollectively to...restore things. Taylor, thoughtsbecoming a member of me kind out anythingdifficultygoes on with the children. You however, do take a **stroll** off the grounds, I don't care what **takes place** out there" He says giving me a **understandingappearance**. He **wishes** me to wipe **the** **man** out...I've **constantlydesired** to **try this** to this **man**...It made my **coronary heart** race with excitement. "I am **now no longer** going with you" He growls. "Scared" I **stated** playfully as we **stroll** out the door, he groans and follows me, his masculinity getting the **higher** of him, **looking** to over-**strength** me. We **strollquick** to **the** **threshold** of the **faculty** border as we get into the treeline surrounding it. "That's **a** **wayssufficient**" He says as I **pay attention** a **click on** of a gun, turning **round** slowly. "What...What are you doing?" I stammer, pretending like I **become** scared. "You realize...I **realize** you do..." He says. "Know what? I'm **simplyright** hereto **return back** to the gala! We **got** **heredomestic** to **go** to. I got here to **go to** my households graves **and are** availableaid the **facultyof** their gala." I say as he lowers the gun slightly. "You're telling me **you don't have anyconcept** what your grandfather did?" He says the gun now down **through** his side. "He **become** in **safety** if that's what you mean. Seriously, **positioned** the gun away! I'm **now no longer** a fucking terrorist!" I cry out. "Shit..." He says **setting** the gun in his holster as I **strolltoward** him. "What's going on?" I ask **as though** I haven't **were given** a clue, shaking my hand slightly, pretending to be scared. "There's **loads** you don't **realize**. There are **guys** after you. They **need** to...to **own** you. Use your **call** as leverage" He says. "Who? What? Why?" I ask. "I **should** die for telling you this Samantha!" He growls out kicking a stone. "Die?! Who's going to kill you? Tony I don't understand!" I cry out, gripping his shoulder. "Shit...There's a **manreferred** to as Hayden he's paying me **cash** to **maintainan** eye fixed on Henderson. He **desires to** take over your grandfathers gang. I don't **realize** details. But he **desires to** use you. I can't stand you Samantha, **however** you don't deserve it...Run, don't come **returned**, hide, **some thing**. Just **go away**!" Tony says. "Shit Tony, I **desire** you weren't **part** of this" I sigh. He **advised** me the truth...But I couldn't **believe** him **now no** longer to rat me out... "What?" His eyes widen on the gun I pull on him. "I realize who I am. I'm the chief of The Midnight Rose. Hayden is coming after my family, huh? Wants to take over?" I growl out. "You knew! Please Samantha! I won't say a aspect I swear! I simply did it for the cash. Please! Hayden wishes you useless, he desires to take the whole lotyou've got got! I can assist you!" He begs. "I'm sorry Tony. But I can't chance my family" I say earlier thantaking pictures him withinside the head, wincing on the sound of the shot earlier than dragging him into the closest bush for his frame to be picked up and carted out of right here. The bush become a rose bush...Now blood-soaked roses. What a super omen.

Chapter Four

Sam to all: Hayden isn't always a friend! Watch your backs! Henderson isn't always an enemy! Sam to Beck: Clean up wishedout of doorsfaculty, framewithinside thetimber south of the gates, rose bush 1/3 from left. Beck: Please inform me you're joking approximately Hayden... Clean up may be done. Sam to Beck: No joke, watch your again! Beck: Yes Ma'am. I holster my gun yet again and make my manneragain to the facultyensuringthere has been no blood on me as I word Taylor and Henderson nearing the office. "Everything sorted?" Henderson says as I nod. "Tonight may be interesting" Taylor sighs as we take a seat down down. "We wantto hold on pretending which yourecognizenot anythinghowever what Lizzy has advised you." Henderson says. "He's coming after me...Why is it usually me?" I sigh, my head in my hands. "You're a effective girl. You'll usually have a personlooking what's yours. But there are humansat the back of you. You simplywant to be cautious in who you believe" Henderson says. "And I idea I shouldbelieve Hayden, appearancein which that were given me..." I sigh. "It's now no longer easy, I apprehendhoweverthis is why you've got gothumans like myself, your different grandfather, Beck and your guysthrough your side. They will **shield** you as **you'llshield** them" He adds. "I **must** wipe Hayden out...Do **you suspect** Lizzy is **aware of?**" I face Taylor. "I don't **recognize**...She **shouldwithout** problems be manipulated...But the **appearance** in her eyes, she doesn't **need** to **harm** you Sammy..." Taylor says. "Shit...We get Hayden, take him out. Take Craig out too **even as** we're at it. We'll **keep** Lizzy, see how she is...If she's being manipulated...I can't...I **recognize** what she's been **thru** Taylor..." I cry. "We'll **address** it. I'll **holda watch** on her." Taylor nods. "I taught your mother, you **recognize**. You're like her **loads** Samantha. She'd be proud" Henderson says as I smile with a tear in my eye. "Thank you. I **wantto name** my boys. Taylor...If this **is going** wrong, you get out, head **domestic** and **shield** my child" I say as he **seems** at me with **ache** in his eyes **earlier than** sighing and nodding. "Nothing **goes** to **occur** to you Sam, **now no longer** on my watch" He says as I hug him earlier **thanputting** off my **telecellsmartphone** and heading **out of** doors. I ring Jayden. "Hey **infant,** I didn't **assume** a **name** so early. Everything ok?" He asks, **the concernclean** in his voice. "Just **a bitfearfulapproximatelythis night**. I desired to pay attention your voices" I stated. "You'll be pleasant Sam. Hey buddy, do you needto speak to mummy?" Jayden says and I smile whilst Cody involves the telecellsmartphone. "Mummy!" Hey giggles happily. "Hi infant boy, how are you? Are you having a laugh with daddy and the others?" I ask. "Yeah! But Uncle Shaun and Uncle Luka now no longerdomestic...they busy" He says sadly. "Busy doing what?" I ask. "I dunno, stuff. Uncle Bwian long past too" he cries. "I'm positivethey'll be again soon" I say. "I leave out you mummy, whilst you come domestic?" He asks. "Soon infant, soon" I solutionattemptingnow no longer to cry. "Daddy needto speak. Love you mummy" He says. "Love you too infant boy" I solution. "So, uhh, the boys...I don't have anyconceptin which they are..." Jayden says coming again to the telecellsmartphone. "What do you suggest you don't recognizein which they are?! You're all imagined to be shielding Cody!" I cry angrily. "There are masses of humansnevertheless here" He says. "I want you to be cautious, Hayden isn't always with us" I say quietly. "WHAT?" he exclaims. "Henderson has been shielding me for years for my mother. Hayden wishes me and my mafia. He changed intopals with my grandfather. Tonight I've were given to take him and Craig down" I sigh. "No...Come domestic, proper now" He says sternly. "I can't simplydepart now! What approximately Henderson? What approximately Beck? What approximately all people?! With Hayden neverthelessroundwe're all in danger! I want you to touch the others and warn them. Anything shouldoccuronce I take down Hayden" I snap again. "You'll die! We'll run we'll crosssomeplace new. Just don't try this Sam!" He cries out. "I don't have any choice. This has to stop, or he's going tohold coming after me. So many humanswerebeneathneath him from the beginning, Vern, Gregory and my Uncle Karlos being a few. This has to stop to hold our own circle of relatives safe! I actually have Taylor, Henderson and Beck, I'll be ok" I say. "Please kitten, I'm begging you, come domestic" He cries. "I can't. I'm sorry Jayden. I love you and Cody so much, keep in mind that. Keep him safe, I'll be domestic soon" I say. "I love you Kitten, come domestic to us. We love you" He whispers sadly. "I'll see you soon. Stay safe. Give Cody masses of hugs for me" I say. "I will" He answers. "Love you, I'll name you whilst it's over" I stated. "You higher kitten. Tell Taylor he'll be in hasslewhen you have a unmarried hair out of location" He says, and I snort. "I will. Bye infant" I say as he says good-bye and we grasp up. I sigh and again up onto a tree as I sob a bit. "Get your selfcollectively Samantha" I say to myself as I wipe my eyes and crossagain indoors. The bells had long past, and youngsters flooded the corridors, I watched the hustle and bustle, remembering once Ichanged intomore youthful and changed into a pupil here. The noises, the smells, it introducedsuch a lot ofrecollectionsagain. I ignored the easier times, however I wouldn't take some thingagain. I cherished my own circle of relatives and might do some thing I should to hold them safe. "Taylor has long past to the auto he's looking forward to you there. I've installation a room for you each to get preparedwithinside the east wing, Taylor is aware ofin which to cross. I'll see you this night Samantha" Henderson makes me jump, creeping up beside me as he used to do as I snort nervously. "Thank you...For everything" I say as I lay my hand on his arm and head againout of doors. "I don't assume Damien could be verysatisfied with our scenarioproper now Sammy" Taylor seems upset. "Neither is Jayden. He stated you highermake certain I don't come domestic with even a hair out of location or you're in deep hassle" I smirk nervously. "Damien stated a comparableissuehowever that neither people are to return backdomesticharm" He hugs me tightly. "We'll get thru this" I say hugging him again. "Of route we will. We usually do"

Chapter Five

"You appearancelovely in that get dressed Samantha" Taylor smiles as I've completed getting ready, my hair is curled round my face, 1/2 of pinned up even as a black lace masks covers 1/2 of of my face, framing my eyes. "Thanks, you appearance great" I smile even assearching at his masks, a pink plastic 1/2 ofmasks which covers the properfacet of his face. "It's time to pass" He holds out an arm to escort me out of the room as my hand shakes a touch. "We can do thatproper?" I say. "We'll be fine. We can do that" He says however I observe the wavering in his voice. The grounds had beenblanketed in little fairy lights, it appeared magical. We entered via the the frontdoorways as I grew to becomeat the coms hyperlinkcautiously in my ear. "It seems gorgeous" I gasp as we input the corridor, it wereadorned with a vibrantpink rose theme. Mr Henderson you sneaky devil...He changed into doing this in my honour. Taylor smiles and nods, main me into the room. "We're right here Sam" Beck says via the hyperlink. "Us too" Lizzy says. "Great. Be cautious out there. I actually have Henderson" I say as I observe Henderson greeting human beings, the handiestguynow no longer in a masks. "Good night! And who would possiblywe've gotright here?" He says to us, shaking our palms. "Just little ole me Mr Henderson" I laugh, gambling along. "Samantha! You appearanceremarkable! Taylor, that can't be you below there can it?" His eyebrows improve in mock marvel as they shake palms laughing. "This vicinityseemslovely" I smile. "Thanks. It could be a night time to remember. Would you return back with me a moment? I would love to introduce you to 3capability investors. I'm certain they'll like tolistena number of your talesapproximatelyresidingright here" He says with a grin as we observe him. He leads us to 3men leaning towards a make-shift bar that wereplaced up for the night. "Ah, gentlemen, I'd want to introduce Samantha Jones, former scholarright here" He says. "Good night Miss Jones, my call is Becker" he smiles as I recognise who it changed into, Beck. "Nice to satisfy you Becker" I smile as he's taking my hand and kisses it. "Quite the gentleman" Henderson laughs. "Who are the guys beside you Becker?" I ask as I observesome thing oddly familiar. "This is Louis, Ben and Sam. They paintings for me" He says with a grin. But he sees the anger in my eyes. Of course, Luka, Brian and Shaun had beenright here... Re-naming them changed intosmart though, as now no longer to spook Hayden into understanding my crewhad beenright here. "Nice to satisfy you boys" Taylor says, his eyes narrowing on them as they fidget. "Excuse me, however did I listen that Samantha Jones is right here?" A guy towers us as he interrupts. "Yes, can also additionally I ask why?" Beck asks, eyeing the person up and down. "I knew her grandfather. We had beenvintage friends. I'd very similar toto speaktogether along with herapproximately him" He says however his eyes consciousness on mine...Hayden... "I'm afraid with the intention to be a touchhard as she's simply agreed to bop with me" Luka says arising to me, taking my hand and main me to the dance ground as his hand brushes my ear and turns off my coms. "What the fuck are you doing?" I say as we sluggish dance, my head in his neck. "You assume I'm going to permit my sister cope with this on my own. That changed into Hayden, I'm certain of it" He growls. "I understand it is. You're going to get us caught. He is aware of all of us. He'll observe there are human beingslooking me" "He will simplyassumewe'remaintaining you safe, however I don't assume he is aware of it's us" He says. "You mustpermit him take me off somewhere. I can't do that in right here. Half the scholars are in right here" I say searchingacross the busy room. Students crammed the bigcorridor as they danced with among the investors. "I'm now no longer leaving you on my own with him whilst he desires to kill you" He says sternly. "You don't have any choice. You ought to be lower backdomesticshielding my son. He nevertheless has guys in MY college" I snap. "Tobias is flawlesslyable to sorting that" He says. "Excuse me, do you thoughts if I take this subsequent dance?" A hand faucets Luka's shoulder and he glares at the person. No concept of who he is. "Of course, the tunechanged intosimply ending" I stated taking the second one mans' hand. "You appearanceremarkable Samantha" He says as I investigate his eyes. "Who are you?" I ask, my eyes dancing over his face. "Zane..." He solutions as I gasp. "Do now no longerappearance now however Hayden is on yourproper. You wantto go away Sam, I didn't recognise he changed into going after you, I swear, or I'd in no wayhad beenpart of this. He instructed me he changed into doing this to hold you safe...But I heard some thing..." He says in a rush. "What is he doing?" I ask, eyes flicking fast to my proper as I noticed him. Hayden changed intostatus beside Lizzy and Craig. Lizzy's eyes had been darting round nervously as they determined mine. "He's going to blow the entirecollege" He says as my eyes bore into his. "What...No" I gasp as my eyes float over the entire crowd in a panic. "When Henderson is goingas much as do his speech at nine, he's going to take Lizzy and his guys out the lower back and blow the vicinity" He says. "Why are you telling me this?" I ask. "I won't have you ever die. You don't deserve it" He solutions. "The kids...Everyone right here...The college...We mustforestall him" I say. "There's not anythingwe will do." He sighs. "Zane, take Lizzy, get her out" I order, and he seems at me extensive-eyed. "But...What approximately you?" He asks. "I'll cope with it" I say as his eyes sadden. "No, no way" He says as his grip tightens. "I'm now no longer letting all of us die" I snarl. "And I won't have Cody lose his mother" He snaps lower back. "What approximately my brother? Shaun?

46

Taylor? Brian? Beck? They are all **right here** too. Should I lose them too?" I say and he **seems** at me, sighs and swears **below** his breath. I **study** the clock **at the** wall, it **changed into** 8.45pm. I had fifteen **mins** to **parent** this out **earlier than** the **vicinity** blew. I took myself from Zane's grip as he **attempted** to **maintain** me harder. "Zane, take her and **pass.** I **mustkeep** them" I **stated** sternly shaking **loose** from him as I **flip** and **stroll** off **closer to** the bathrooms, turning on my com **hyperlink.** "Little Samantha, how **cuteto peer** you" Hayden rounds the **nookin the back of** me, taking my arm with a grin. "Fuck...Hayden...Didn't **count onto peer** you **right here**" I gasp playfully as I **listen** Lizzy in my ear. "I didn't **recognise,** I swear Sam" She whispers. "What's the plan Hayden? You knew my grandfather? You **need** what's mine? So many have come after me for it. So why right here? Why **pass** after Henderson?" I ask as **he's taking** of his **masks** throwing it to the **floor** with a **extensive** grin. "Your grandfather **changed intoan awesomepal** of mine. Louisa **changed intoimagined to** be mine, I paid for her, **however** he **permit** Gregory have her. Then she ran off with Trent and had you. I knew **you will** be the key. Smart, talented, **lovely**, I **desired** my daughter to have the best. But, **the kidchanged into** NOT the plan. So, I driven her and **driven** her, drove her **loopytill** she took **the kid**. You **had beenimagined to** be baron. No children, **damaged** like Lizzy and **clean** to control. But **whenever** you get out of my clutches!" He shouts, pushing me **towards** the wall, punching it **close to** my face. "So now what? Am I **not** any good?" I say as he grabs my arm dragging me painfully, **viaa chain** of **doorways**. "You going to blow the **vicinity**? Is that it?" I say, hoping they heard me **via** the coms. "I will **very own** you. Kill **all of us** you love, **spoil** you piece **with the aid of using** piece **till** I can **mildew** you to my **very own** vision." He smirks and brings out a button. "No! You don't **must** blow the **college**! I'll **include** you, **simply** don't blow it!" I cry out. "Get **all of us** out!" Beck shouts in my ear. "Let's watch the fireworks shall we?" He grins, **getting rid of** the **protection** cover. "What **approximately** Lizzy? She's in there **proper**? You'd kill your **very own** daughter?!" I cry out **seeking toforestall** him as he brings a gun to my head. "My daughter is WEAK! You'll be **a lot** better. I've **visible** you in action, I can experiencethe fadinterior you! I'll use that for my advantage. People will cower in fear!" He shouts. "Don't fucking contact her" Zane creeps in the back of him placing a gun to Hayden's head. "Well, well, well, I puzzled if you willsurrender the game. Which is why I had your sister come right here too. She's with Craig proper now" Hayden grins as Zane's maintain faulters. "No!" Zane shouts angrily as I attempt to wipe out Hayden's legs, he drops the button and I attempt toforestall it from urgenttowards the floor as Zane's gun shoots' at Hayden however misses. They get right into a scramble at thefloor as Hayden kicks him difficultwithinside the stomach, searching at me earlier than running. "This isn't the end!" He growls. "No!" I scream because the button hits the floor. Hayden makes a run for it as he darts into the trees, entering into an watching forautomobilebecause it speeds off. It's just like theentireinternational is in sluggish motion, flames erupt from the floor as we're tossed backwards from the explosion. Splinters of wooden hit us, reducing our arms, rocks exploded round us and the college is up in flames as I listen the screams. "What has he done?"

Lizzy's voice whispers angrily in the back of me as she runs out from in the back of a automobile. "Taylor!" I scream out. "Shaun! Brian! Luka!!" I scream all over again as I run closer to the building. "No! You can't pass in! You'll burn!" Zane holds me lower back, grunting on theache of his ribs. "I mustlocate them!" I scream as I combattowards his maintain. "They're long gone Sam" He repeats preserving me lower back as I scream. Next Chapter

Chapter Six

"Sam!" A voice shouts, coughing loudly from the proper of the hearthplace ridden constructing as I push out of Zane's grip, strolling in my heels, closer to the voice. "Luka!" I cry as I leap into his fingers, sobbing. "I notion he took you!" He cried wrapping his fingersround me. "The others? Where are they?" I sob searchingat the back ofto peerhuman beings being dragged out of the constructing. "I don't recognise Sam we have beencut up up. We have beenlooking to get all people out. I haven't located any of them" He says, his eyes packed withache. "Sam, you're shaking" Zane comes up at the back of me. "Help them! Luka assist them get the oneshuman beings out. Lizzy! Call the emergency services!" I shout ordering them as they nod and get to it. My get dressedchanged intoreduce to portions, however I didn't care. I rushed roundsupportingthose whohave beennonethelesspopping out the constructing. People with burns, cuts, bruises and a few who have been being dragged out dead. I observedhuman beingssuffering from simplyinner as I ran closer to them to assist. "Beck!" I shout as I see him dragging a frameat the back of him. "Don't Sam!" He shouts as I come closer. "No!" I scream as I be aware who it changed into. Taylor laid nonetheless in his fingers as he dragged him out of the constructing. Burns protected his stunningframe as we were given him out. "Beck, inform me he's alive!" I cry out. "I'm running on it!" He growls, doing CPR. "Taylor!" I cry out in ache. "No, come on kid!" Beck shouts. Fire engines flip up as they get to paintings on calming the raging fires. Paramedics flit thru the crowds of human beings. Deciding who they mightstore, a few weren't so lucky. "Sam, movelocate Shaun. You don't want to be right here" Beck orders angrily. "I'm now no longer leaving him!" I say gripping Taylor's hand, however his pores and skinactionsbeneathbecause it comes farfar from his hand slightly, the burn had performedquite a fewharm. My hand changed intoprotected in his blood as I cried out. "Go!" Beck shouts at me angrily as I shake. "Come on" Zane alternatives me up from the floor making me stroll away. "No...Taylor..." I cry as his fingerssurround me. "Luka!" Zane shouts as he spots my brother. "Whose blood is that?" He factors to my palms. "T...T...Taylor" I cry. "Have you located the others?" Zane asks sitting me subsequent to Lizzy as she sits quietly, her eyes flicking over the destruction. "No. Not Henderson, Shaun, Brian or maybe Craig" Luka shakes his head as I sob. "Not my boys…" I sob. "Sam, you're bleeding" Lizzy says seeking to my aspect. "What?!" Luka notices the blood seeping from my aspect. "It's only areduce, it's now no longer deep" Zane says checking. "Excuse me, I'm searching out a Samantha Jones, do you realizein which she is probably?" A paramedic asks "That's me" I say as she leads me to an ambulance quickly. "The firefighters located him with an extraguyclose to the lower back of the constructing." She states and shall we me see who'swithinside the ambulance. "Shaun!" "Sam" He groans "It's ok. You're ok" I say kissing his head. "Brian…He took the hit…The beam got here down…He…" He coughed up blood. "No…now no longer him too" I cry. "I couldn't store him" Shaun sobs. "Shh, you figure on getting your self better. I'll be there quickly ok. I ought tolocate Henderson. Luka's out and so are Zane and Lizzy. Taylor…He's…I don't recognise…He wasn't breathing, his burns…Beck instructed me to go away" I cry. "Tell Elise…I love her…" Shaun says coughing earlier than passing out. "You've were givento move we want to take him NOW!" The paramedic stated as she shoved me out and that they raced off. My palmshave been shaking, how may want to he have performed this? All the kids, all of thehuman beings he changed into killing, due to me... Fire combatantshave been bringing out our bodies as I walked up slowly to them, searchingon the faces. "No..." I sobbed after Ilocated I recognised...Zara and Brian. "No!" I screamed falling to my knees, my palms on their fingers, keeping on for expensive life. "Samantha!" Zane ran up and located me. "Zane don't!" I stand preventing him from seeing his sister at thefloor, however it changed into too late. "No! Not my sister! Not Zara!" He shouts angrily. "Zane, don't, don't appearance" I stated dragging him farfar from the our bodies as he sobbed. "Oh no! Not Zara!" Lizzy regarded to us as Zane fell to the floor. "Lizzy deal with him" I stated as she nodded and hugged him tightly as he sobbed into her fingers. I regarded to in which Beck and Taylor had been, however they have beenlong past. Please permit him be ok... Henderson, in whichchanged into Henderson? "Sam! I located Henderson!

What happened? Who?" Luka checked out my distraught face, taking my head in his palms. "Brian, Zara... Shaun's harm badly, I don't recognise how Taylor is..." I cry as Luka takes me in his fingers. "We'll get thru this. One step at a time" He mumbles into my hair, however I pay attention the sorrow in his voice. "Samantha!" Henderson runs as much as us and takes eachpeople into his fingers. "If you hadn't of stated what you probably did and while you did...we'd all be dead...Thank you" He says. "Brian's dead, Zara's Dead, Taylor is probably dead, Shaun is probably dying...There are nonethelesssuch a lot ofhuman beings to be located...Because my own circle of relatives...He'll pay for this" I start. "No don't you dare blame your self. This isn't always your fault. Do now no longer blame your self for this. You will move, see your palswithinside the hospital, you'llcollecteach fibre of your braveness and get on as you continually have. Command appreciate and be together along with yourown circle of relatives. I will addressthe autumn out right hereand phone you after I can. Now move!" Henderson says shoving Luka and I away. "Thank you" I stated as Luka takes my hand as we take hold of Zane and Lizzy from the floor, dragging them to our car. "Beck!" I shout as we arrive on the hospital, he's pacing the emergency room ready room as we burst thru the doors. "Did you locate Brian?" He asks. "He's long past" I cry. "Fuck!" He growls as he sits down, his head in his palms. "Taylor?" I ask as he shakes his head. "No...inform me he's now no longer..." I sob kneeling in the front of him. "They don't suppose he's going to make it..." He mumbles. "Shaun? Did you notice him?" Luka asks. "Surgery, the beam beaten him and Brian, Brian took the overall force, saving Shaun" Beck answered. "We wantto name the others" Luka places a hand on my shoulder. "I...I...I don't suppose I can..." I cry. "Yes you can, you're the most powerfullady ever. They want to recognise Sam. But in case you can't, I'll do it. My father did this..." Lizzy says taking my hand as she held Zane in her lap. I nod and take my telecellsmartphone from the pocket in my get dressed and byskip it to her. "I can't do it...I...I wantto move for a stroll...Come get me if there's an update" I order as all of them nod. I wandered thru the halls as I noticedincreasingly morehuman beings from the explosion, human beings with terrible burns, a few with portions of constructingof their sides, screaming, shouting and crying. I needed toget out! I ran out of doors into the bloodless air as I sat in a darkishnookout of doors, sitting on a small wall. "Sammy?" Lizzy's faint voice calls out as she sits beside me and places her head in opposition to mine. "I can't do that anymore...I can't" I cry. "Yes you can. You can do that. We can all do that" She says taking my shaking hand in hers and pulling me up. "We want to get your aspectchecked out" She says main me inner as she calls over a nurse who takes me right now to appearance over my wounds. Within 1/2 of an hour I'm stitched up and readywithinside theready room with the others as we wait to pay attention anything. "Miss Jones?" A nurse comes thru. "Yes!" I stand. "Come with me" She says as I observe her. She leads me to a room off the aspect as we input I see Taylor, his frameprotected with bandages. "Taylor!" I cry out as I rush to his aspect. He changed intononetheless breathing, however it changed into erratic. "S...Sa...Saam" He stutters, wincing on theache. "Shh, I've were given you. Hold on Taylor. Hold on" I cry. I can't contact him he's protected in burns.

"Look...Lo...appearance...After...Damien"
He stammers. "No, you're going to do that.
Hold on Taylor. Please, I can't lose you
too!" I'm complete on sobbing.
"B...Be...Brave..." He says. "Not with out
you. I can't do that Taylor! I mustin no
way have taken you there. We must have
long past home!" I cry.
"N...Not...Your...Fault" He says. "Taylor. I
swear in case yougo away me, I'm going
to return backonce you myself" I growl in
tears. "Lov...Love...you" He says earlier
than his framestarts offevolved to shake,
alarms ring as nurses shove me out the
room, I'm screaming. "No! Taylor! Don't
go away me!" I scream. "Come on!" Beck
holds me tightly, dragging me from the
room however I elbow him and break out
his clutches as I press in opposition to the
glass as I watch them paintings on my
excellentbuddy. I watch as they forestall.
"Time of death, ten fifty-three" The
medical doctor says as I burst in
screaming for them now no longer to
forestall as Beck grabs me as soon as
more, pinning my fingers to my aspect.
"Just as soon as more! Please" I scream as
a medical doctor takes pity on me and
agrees, attemptingas soon as more. "Holy
Shit!" The medical doctor cries as Taylor's

machines beep as soon as more, he changed into alive! "Get her out of right hereat the same time as we paintings!" A nurse shouts as they start topaintings on him. Beck drags me out of the room and lower back into the readyvicinity as he locations me in my brothers lap. "What happened?" Luka asks. "He died...He changed into dead, however she screamed at them to attemptas soon as more...They were given him lower back after maintaining him dead" Beck says pacing. "He can't die...Not now...Not ever...He's my excellentbuddy" I murmur into Luka's blouse as he strokes my hair to calm me down. An hour, an hour is how lengthy it took for me to calm sufficient to pay attention what changed intotaking placeround me. My coronary heartharm, it changed into shattered into portions, Brian changed into dead, and the ladshave beennonetheless in trouble, as some othermedical doctorgot herethru. "Are you the own circle of relatives of Shaun Beckett?" He asks "Yes" Beck nods. "We were given him thru the surgery, however I'm afraid the harmchanged into extensive...He'll in no waystroll again. He's paralysed from the waist down. He'll wake quickly. If a persondesires to see him" The medical doctor says as Beck thank you him. "Sam? Do you needto peer him?" Luka asks as I nod sniffling. They lead me to the room in which Shaun is connected to numerous machines as I take a seat downsubsequent to his bed, taking his hand in mine. "We'll go away you with him for a at the same time as" Beck nods as I relaxation my head on Shaun's hand. "You've were given to wake up, I want you" I cry. "Sam..." His voice calls out gruffly as my head shoots up to fulfill his. His eyes looking mine. "Where's Taylor? Brian?" He asks "Taylor's terrible...We misplaced him as soon as...I...He won't make it. Brian's... dead" I sob as his hand tightens in mine. "I'm sorry...He's strong...He has to make it" He murmurs, a tear in his eye from dropping a valuablebuddy of ours. "It's now no longer your fault" I shake my head. "It's now no longer yours either" He says looking my face. "Shaun...You...You're...You're paralysed" I spit out. "I notion as much. I can't sense them, my legs...But...I'm alive...That's the principlecomponentproper?" He says his hand squeezing mine. "I want to get the medical doctor" I stated as I kiss his head, my eyes have been sore from crying so much. My **coronary heart** heavy from **ache** as he watches me **go away** the room. "Um...Doctor...He's awake" I **stated** to the **medical doctor** who **were given** us in **advance** as he nods and enters the room.

Chapter Seven

I wander aimlessly via the corridors, now no longerunderstandingin which my toeshad been taking me as I become outside, sitting on a brick wall, leaning my head returned, searchingon the stars above me. "Mummy!" I pay attention as my eyes dart toward the sound. "Cody" I breathe out as I run to them and take him in my fingers as I fall to my knees. "Kitten!" Jayden embraces eachpeople as I'm hugged tighter than I had ever been earlier than. "Sam?" Damien's voice calls out at the back of them as my eyes dart to his. "Damien!" I cry as I burst from my own circle of relatives's fingers and visit him. "Taylor...Where is he?" He appears into my eyes, as they cloud over with tears again. "No...He's now no longer...Tell me he's now no longer..." He grips me tough as I see worry flood his face.   "He...He's terrible...Burns...Everywhere...He flatlined...I screamed at them to preserve going, they declared him lifeless...I screamed, and that theyattemptedas soon asgreater...He got herereturned...He got herereturned" I cry as he is taking me into his fingers sobbing. "I want to discover him. Thank you...Thank you for making them **attempt** again" He says as he rushes in **doorways** as I **pay attention** him shouting at my brother to **discoverin** **which** Taylor is. "Mummy sad…" Cody tugs on my battered **get dressed**. "My grandbaby!" Grandpa rushes **as much as** me with Savannah and Elise **warm** on his tail as he hugs me to him. "Luka?" Savannah mumbles **searching** at me, her eyes drifting over my **get dressed** and the blood I **becomeincluded** in. "He's alive, he's **interior**" I say as she kisses my cheek and runs **interior**. "Sammy…Where is Shaun?" Elise whispers taking my hand. "He **were** **given** hurt…Brian took **maximum** of the damage…Brian died saving Shaun…" I sob as **all of them** gasp. "Uncle Bwian in sky wit daddy?" Cody cries. "Yes **infant, there has been** a **terrible** accident. Uncle Brian with daddy **withinside the** sky" I sob as he jumps into my **fingers** as we sob. Elise **is goingto** **stroll** in **earlier than** I take her arm. "There's **some thing** else isn't there?" She mumbles as I nod. "He…He's paralysed from the waist down" I say as she gasps and rushes off into the hospital. "Kitten…Let's **passinterior**, it's **bloodless** out here" Jayden takes my hand as I **maintain** Cody to me tightly as we head into the **ready** room. "What the bloody hell **passed off**?" Lindsey asks as she sits **subsequent** to me and Grandpa. "Hayden **wishes** me...He's been **towards** us all this time **due to the fact** he **desires to** use me as a weapon, he **wishes** me **vulnerable** so he can **manage** me" I cry. "He's **in no way** touching you again" Lizzy grumbles as she strokes Zane's hair in her lap. "Damn **proper**..." Jayden growls. "Tell me everything, I **want** to **replace** Tobias. We've already **were given** the **faculty** on **excessive** alert. Some of Hayden's **guys** have **positioned** down their **weapons** already claiming **that they'd** no idea. But **we've** them locked up **simply** in case" Grandpa says. "We'll **determine** it out. Shaun **could be** ok, and Taylor will live on this..." Luka says. "Why the fuck **had been** you there anyway! You weren't **prepurported** to be there! You **had beenprepurported** to be defensive my son!" I shout passing Cody whimpering to Jayden, storming **as much as** my brother. "You **wantedreturned** up" He says **not** able to **appearance** me in **the attention**. "And I had it! Beck **become** there! And Henderson! Why couldn't you **simplylivein** which you **had beenprepurported** to, then Shaun and

Brian couldwere fine!" I scream at him as I pay attention Cody whimper loudly at the back of me. "Mummy no shout" Cody whimpers in Jayden's fingers. "I'm sorry infant boy, mummy's upset" I say stroking his head and kissing it. "Mummy pass over uncle bwian" He sobs. "Yes infant" I cry. "Let's go away the talks approximately what passed offtill after the kids are in bed" Beck says with a nod, however I glare at my brother as he shrinks into the nook with Savannah in his fingers. Damien walks into the room shaking an hour later as he collapses in the front of me, sitting among my legs as he sobs into his palms. "He's so burnt...He's in a coma...They positioned him in a coma..." He sobs as I maintain his hand cuddling him round his shoulders. "He's nevertheless here, he instructed me to appearance after you, he loves you Damien, he won't go away. Not now" I say preserving him tight as he keeps to shake. "I'm so sorry Sam" Lizzy whispers searchingon thehuman beingsround us. "Why is she here?" Jayden growls in my ear. "Because it become her dad that did this, and he's been manipulating her all this time. She desires us Jay..." I appearance him in the attention as I see the battle in his eyes as he darts among her and Cody. "I'll do higherwith out him...I'm sorry I did what I did...I wasn't in my proper mind...Zane will assist me...He usually had earlier than" She says as Zane nods, his head now on her shoulder. "I'll make certain she remainsat theimmediately and narrow. You want us Sam. I want revenge for my sister" He says, the mildlong past from his eyes. "This is a joke..." Jayden growls. "Enough" I snap, seeking tomake certain Cody remains asleep in my fingers after he had sobbed for thus long. "Samantha..." Mr Henderson sneaks into the room as all eyes land on him. "Henderson..." I whimper as I see him included in blood and ash. "Your friends?" He asks. "Shaun's paralysed, Brian and Zara are lifeless and Taylor...He's in a terriblemanner" I say as he nods solemnly. "More human beingscould have died this nightin case you hadn't of known as out..." He says. "May I ask who the fuck you're?" Grandpa growls. "Dreadfully sorry, I'm Mr Henderson, Abraham in case you like. I'm the top of the faculty that becomesimply blown to pieces. I've watched over Samantha for years, pretty the youngerfemale she's come to be. You are?" He holds out a hand to my Grandpa as they shake. "Harvey Jennings, her grandfather" Grandpa says and Henderson's eyes flicker over us each. "I've heard lotsapproximately you sir, you'recertainly a higher grandfather than Jon become" Henderson sits with the aid of using Beck as they shake palms too. "Doesn't take an awful lot" I smirk as there's a small chortlewithinside the room. "Has anybody been capable oftune what passed off to Hayden?" Henderson asks. "Zane and I were givenright into acombat with him as he dropped the button...He excessive-tailed it right into aautomobile and vanished...Can't say I've had the threat to discover him yet...Been a bit busy" I snap "That's no tone to apply Samantha" Henderson says sternly. "Sorry sir" I bow my head because the others have a take a observe me in shock. "How the fuck did you do that? No one shuts her down like that..." Savannah laughs. "Being her precept for prettysome years has its benefits. I'm prettyinformedapproximately her temper swings and the way tofight her" Henderson smirks. "What age become she the worse?" Savannah asks as I groan. "Oh I could say thirteen. She had pretty the mood going into her teenage years...I in particulardo not forget her entering my workplaceincluded in a fewkind of slime after an test she did in technological know-how, made pretty the mess" He smiles. "THAT become an accident!" I laugh. I had combinedthe incorrectchemical substancesat some point in technological know-howafter which boom! A gooey substance included the room as women had shrieked and the men laughed. "But you loved it... I do do not forget the appearance of pleasurewhilst you did it, in particularwhile Lisa got here out in a insteadterrible rash" He says. "Samantha!" Grandpa booms laughing. "She deserved that! She bccomenot anythinghoweveran uncongenial queen wannabe!" Henderson started out sharing greatertalesapproximately me and Taylor returned at faculty as they laughed, we had had prettysome shenanigans in our time. But then it have become serious. "Do you do not forget your first gala you went to Samantha?" Henderson asks. "Yeah, I become Fourteen. Grandpa Jon were given me this actually gross get dressed, it become pink, and I hated it. I destroyed it and stated it become an accident. He were given so mad. I locateda brand newget dressed myself with Taylor and he didn't approve of it. But, he dragged us across the gala and added me to such a lot ofhuman beings, it made my head dizzy. Little did I recognise, he becomeseeking to pawn me off" I grumble. "I accept as true with Hayden become there that night…" He says as I boost my head toward his. I try todo not forget the gala, absolutely everyone I met. "Oh my god…So had been you!" I stated pointing to Lizzy. I remembered her crimsonget dressed with a decent little bow on thereturned. "You do not forget that?" She asks. "Barely…" I answer. "Was that the handiest time Lizzy?" Jayden pipes up. "No…There had beenas a minimum3greater we got here too…" She answers. "You had beenlooking her this entire time…" Jayden growls. "I didn't recognise! I simplyconcept she becomesome otherlady who become dragged to their households parties!" She exclaims. "He's been looking me this entire time…" I mumble. "Kitten, are we able topass talk?" Jayden asks as I nod, and he passes Cody to Lindsey. We stroll out the the front as he starts offevolved to get frustrated, his fists stored clenching angrily. "Just spit it out" I snap. "I don't like her **round** us! Her father **wishes** you! How do **you** understand she's **secureround** us! Like **ultimate** time! She **attempted** to kill herself and Cody!" He shouts at me. "Lizzy is what I **should** have **come to be**...If **matters** hadn't have **passed off** the **manner** they did. If Jon had survived I **should** have **come to be** her. I **recognise** she **may be** saved. We'll watch her. She's **additionally** our **excellentwager** to get to Hayden!" I shout **returned**. "I will **now no longerpermit** her **close to** our **own circle of relatives** and that's final!" He growls. "You'll do as you're fucking **instructed** Jayden, I am the **chief** of this mafia, **now no longer** you. She **desiresassist** and she'll get it. I **ought to** get to Hayden. He's destroying everything!" I **look atthe gapand spot** a van sat in park, its **lightingon, I felt as though** we **had been** being watched. "You're going to get **your self** killed" he growls as **he is taking** me in his **fingers**. "Then I'll die **preventing** for the **human beings** I love" I say as he huffs and kisses my head. "Fine she **remainsround**. But she's watched, doesn't come to the **residence** and **remains** the fuck **farfar** from our boy" He says as I nod. "Deal"

"I'm going to headtestat the guys. I become so scared I become going to lose you kitten. I love you" he kisses my lips in short and walks interior as a tear falls from my cheek. "Hello there Samantha" A voice booms from at the back of me as I'm searchingon the van in the front of me even asthe motive forcesimply takes off. I becometargeted on the incorrect vehicle. I whirl round to discover Hayden with a smirk statusfacet-with the aid of using-facet of guys as they take hold of me quick and package me right into aautomobile nearby. I kick and cry out as an awful lot as I can, however it's no use. The emergency room is so busy that no person notices what's occurring outside. The others had been all in doorwaysafter which they positioned a rag on my face as I slowly started out to lose consciousness. Chloroform

Chapter Eight

I slowly wake, my fingers are sure with cable ties, a gag in my mouth and a sequence on my ankle in a darkish room. Where the hell am I? Did the others understand I become taken yet? Or did they suppose I had deserted them? "You're awake...Good..." Hayden seems out of nowhere withinside the darkness as he flicks a transfer and the brilliant luminescent lightingflip on, I'm squinting from the brightness as he perches on a chair nearby, we're separated via way of means of bars from ceiling to ground. I pull the gag from my mouth...Real clevermen...they couldn't even gag me properly. "You'll die for this!" I growl out and he simply laughs as I improve myself from the ground, statusvia way of means of the bars. "I don't doubt you need to kill me proper now. But, you'll be mine quicklysufficient" He smirks as I hit the bars angrily. "I'll in no way be yours" I shout. "You will or I will passlocate your son and damage him. I nonetheless have human beingsbeneathneath cover, your own circle of relatives will in no way get to him in time to shop him Samantha. You could be mine or he's going to die. That's the problem with own circle of relatives

Samantha, they make you weak" He stands gazing me with a snide smirk. "Good good fortune with that, he's were given a bigown circle of relatives, they'll in no wayalloweverybody take him." I snap. "I can't wait to interruptyou Samantha, this may be a laugh! You'll be begging to paintings for me quickly. Tell me you're mine" He says as his fingers come via the bars and I visitchunk him as he touches my cheek and he pulls his hand again laughing. "I'll in no way be yours" I shout. "You will...I supply it per week...You'll be begging me...Pleading for me to prevent what I even have planned...The faster you supplywithinside themuch lessache you'll passvia" He smirks earlier thanstrolling away. "If you harm my own circle of relatives, so assist me god Hayden! I'll rip your fucking throat out!" I shout as he chuckles and leaves. Why did I usuallybecomeabducted in a fucking cement mobileular?! The groundbecome bare, the mobileular had a sink, a rest room and a mattress, a actual small window close to the ceiling that I shouldslightlyattain, it become frosted so I couldn't even see out of it. Jayden mightpreserve Cody secure the others mightdefend him... I scream in frustration because the door opens all over again and Hayden's goons from the autoare available with a smirk. One pulls a gun as the alternative unlocks the door to my mobileular. "Don't even reflect onconsideration on doing some thingsilly" The man with the gun snarls at me. "Don't contact me" I kick the fellowlooking to undo the chain on my ankle as soon as it's launched. He falls again and the person with the gun comes ahead and hits me difficult on the top as I pass down, blood dripping from my head. "I stated DON'T do some thingsilly!" He snarls as they each drag me out, we pass down a chilly corridor, my knees grazing in opposition to the cement of the ground as they pull me into every other room, chucking me in the direction of a vat of water as I'm made to kneel in the front of it. "Be mine" Hayden growls. "Go fuck yourself" I growl againbecause themen take keep of me. "Fine, have it this manner. You will burn out quicklysufficient. Do it" He says as they tip me the other way up and dunk my head into the water as I cry out, the bloodless water nipping at me and my breath misplaced to me as they drown me. Suddenly I'm yanked again out simplyearlier than the factor I might have handed out as I cough up water, it spills out from my mouth, spitting it at the ground. "Be mine" Hayden kneels in the front of me. "You need to kill me don't you...Can't take now no longer getting what's yours. I will in no way be yours" I spit as he indicators for them to do it once more. "You WILL be mine. If it involves the quit of per week and you haven't succumbed to me, I will circulate my guystowards your own circle of relatives and I will take them out one at a timetillyou've got gotnot anything left" He snaps. "Good good fortune with that. You'll in no waycontact them" I cough, my lungs burning. "We shall see. Do it once more" He says because the day consists of on like this numerousinstancesearlier than I byskip out, my intellectual and bodilykingdom exhausted as they chuck me soaking moist and bloodless into the mobileular. "Enjoy the bloodless sweetheart" One of them chuckles and locks the door at the back of him. I handed out at themattress, shivering from the bloodless water that also clung to my skin. I mightin no way bow right all the way down to him. My own circle of relativesmight be secure...Beck and Tobias mightpreserve them alive. We had effective allies, they mightassist...But did he have spies internal...I prayed that Lizzy and Zane weren't involved...They were so actual for a moment... They'd paintings it out...They'd preserve Cody secure... Taylor...Shaun...Oh god they have been out of the game...Could he get to them? No, he wouldn't pass after a person down already...Would he? I become awoken all of suddenvia way of means of a bucket of freezing water being thrown on me as I screamed. Laughter crammed the room as numerousguys stood looking as I shivered. "What the fuck are you searching at?" I shout via the chattering teeth. "She's going to be a laughto interrupt" One smirked starting the mobileular door as others grabbed mo. "I won't fucking spoil asshole" I snap, and that theysimplysnigger dragging me to the room we have been in earlier than. "Samantha, how are you feeling this morning?" Hayden smirks sitting in a chair withinside the corner. "Fucking peachy" I growl. "Ready to be mine yet?" He asks. "I'd as an alternative die" I spit at him. "That may be arranged" he growls storming as much as me as a huge stick presses as much as my throat. "Go on then...Kill me" I gasp for air as he presses harder. "No...I haven't completed with you yet. You'll supply in quickly. Now do you recognize what that is in my hand?" I study his fingers. Fuck it become a livestock prod. "Is that what you want to preserve your guys on their toes?" I answer. His finger presses the button on it as I see the electrical zing throughout the tip. "Your frame will sense this plentyextra than a ordinary person. You're exhausted, moist and absolutely vulnerable. Say you're mine now and this all is going away" he walks as much as me as he continuesurgent the button to scare me...It works, I balk the nearer he gets, however no mannershould I supply in. "I heard it may be pretty arousing" I sneer. "Let's see then shall we" He smirks and brings it right all the way down to my chest as I jolt with ache, crying out. "Aroused yet?" A man says at the back of me as I swing out a leg and he is going down. "Samantha, I will now no longer take you attacking my guys!" Hayden says kicking me difficultwithinside the chest as I pass down, wheezing at theground. "Not my fault they're sillysufficient to live that near me" I snap, as I'm flung again up and onto my knees roughly, a hand crushing my neck. "Let me fucking tear her aside, we don't **want** her Hayden" The **man** who I had kicked says in my ear. "She **could be** mine! Get your **fingers** off of her Marcus" Hayden shouts as Marcus **we could** me **pass**, throwing me to the ground. "Are you ok?" Hayden lifts my chin as I swat it away. "Like you care" I spit. "Seb, take her for a **warmbathe, supply** her a **fewmealsafter** which throw her **againwithinside themobileular**" Hayden huffs and drags Marcus out of the room with the others, all bar one. Why the fuck **might** he **supply** me a **warmbathe** and **meals**? It's like he **become** bi-polar sometimes! "He's **now no longer** that **terrible** to **paintings** for, **you recognize, in case youlive** on his **proper** side" Seb says dragging me to my feet. "I'd **as an alternative** die than **paintings** for him" I growl as he sighs and drags me to a bathroom. "Shower, I'll be staying **properright** here. Don't **reflect onconsideration on** arguing" He says, **reducingthe binds** on my wrists as I roll my wrists **round**. "You're **now no longer** even going **to showround?**" I study him smirking. "And **allow you toariseat** the back of me and wipe me out? No **thank you** princess" He says. "DON'T **name** me princess" I growl... "Hit a nerve have I?"

He smirks and pushes me in the direction of the bathe, he watches closely as I strip quickly. I word his eyes tour down my framebecause thebathe is became on. "Eyes are up right here" I snap as he simply chuckles. "I don't care" He sneers as he keepsto observe me bathe. I wash quickly, the bloodless leaving my frame as I flip the bathe off and he fingers me a towel. He chucks a couple of going for walks bottoms and a vest at me as I get dressedquickly, seeminglybeneathneath-put on wouldn't be needed...At least I hand a few clothing...I guess... "Why the fuck is he doing this? Does he suppose being bestgets to me?" I say as I'm exceeded a sandwich as Seb stares at me with a gun in his hand. "You are higher off simply doing what he says" He says and turns to his telecellsmartphone. I ate the sandwich quickly, now no longer realising how hungry I becomeearlier than he sure my wrists once more and took me again to the mobileular. "See you later princess" He goads "Fuck you!" I scream at him. How the hell become I going to get out of right here? I had paced the mobileular so normallyearlier than Hayden got here in and sat out of doors of attainall over again. "Your pal Taylor wakened this afternoon...Here look" He says displaying an photoat thetelecellsmartphone of Damien sat beside Taylor, tears of happiness on Damien's face. "If you contact them..." I whisper angrily. "Be mine..." Hayden says. "God rattling it! Why ought to I?" I shout smacking the bars. "Your own circle of relativescould besecure. I'll use you for anything I see fit. You're a weapon Samantha, one I need to use. I understand there's a risky weapon on yourcoronary heart, it runs on yourown circle of relatives, I noticed it in Jon, your father and I am positive you keep it on yourpersonalcoronary heart too. Be mine and we'll take the arenavia way of means of storm. Nothing might be untouchable" he grins. "And if I don't?" I say. "Then your own circle of relatives will die, one at a time. I will deliver your babyright here and make you watch as I tear him aside limb from limb" He says as I stumble again. "You contact my own circle of relatives and I'll kill you" "Then be mine!" He snaps. "No fucking manner" I growl. "Fine" He says and storms out. I wish I wasn't gambling this wrong...I was hoping my own circle of relativeshave beensecure. The following couple of days went similar to the first, drowning, ache, bodily torture which handiestwere given worse. His guyswere given worse while he left them on my own with me, fondling my frame as I attempted to combatagain. My framebecomeprotected in bruises from the beatings. My lungs have been sore from them drowning and preventing my breathing. I become exhausted and every day he addeda brand newpicturegraph of my own circle of relativesdisplaying he should get to them. I become weakening from his torture and he knew it as he grinned while getting me from my mattress this morning, dragging me to the room all over again. "Who do you belong to?" He asks as I go searching the room. It become empty... "Myself" I groan as I'm chained from ceiling to ground, stretched out. "I didn't need to mustpass this far." He says bringing out his telecellsmartphoneearlier thancreating a video name as I watched in horror. "Yes boss?" A voice answered, I didn't realise it. "Are you close to the ladies?" Hayden stated with a smirk as I checked out him and the telecellsmartphone wide-eyed as I noticed the photoflip to Savannah, Elise, Tammy, Layla, Louisa and Lizzy all in a setcollectivelyon the park. "No!" I shout.

"Be prepared on my mark" Hayden says as I listenthe pressing of the gun. "No! Don't do that Hayden!" I cry out sufferingin opposition to the chains. "Who do you belong to?" He asks. I don't say a word, my eyes targetedat theladieswithinside the video. "Aim...in 3...2..." He begins. "NO! I'm yours! Don't harm them!" I scream out defeated. "Stand down" He smirks and turns the telecellsmartphone off. "Don't harm them" I cry. "I statedit mighthandiest take per week, we nonetheless have days left. Good female. Release her. Take her to her room" Hayden says as I'm launched from the chains sagging in opposition to the palmsround me. I needed to play this every othermanner...Maybe getting near him and operating my manner from the internal out...I'd play the bestfemale for him...He'd in no way see me fucking coming

Chapter Nine

For the following couple of weeks he simplysaved me in a small bedroom, they made positive I had food, apparel and a bathroom. I becomeevery so oftenlet loose for small tasks, a torturing right here and there, howevernot anythingmassive. I hadn't visible Hayden in some days, and I become pacing in my room. I wanted out I become going loopy in right here. I had no concept what day it become or anything. "Good morning Samantha! How are we doing?" Hayden bursts via the door with a massive grin. "Fucking peachy. Are you going to allow me out a fewfactorquickly or preserve me prisoner?" I snap from the bed. "That's what I'm right here for, I actually have a marvel for you" He grins and gestures for me to observe him. "What is it?" I ask as he stops at a door. "Your birthday treat" He smirks. "My...Birthday...Oh shit" I mumble as he opens the door and he pushes me inside. I stumble withinside the room and withinside the centre is a personsureat thefloor as I slowly strollas much as them. "Who is it?" I ask. "Don't fear Samantha I didn't drag a personyou adore in right hereto be able to kill. This guy is into a few very dodgy business...With **kids**" Hayden smirks giving me a file. Rage fills my eyes and he **shouldnote** it. "Have at it...Happy Birthday Samantha" He smirks **because themanstartsto** **grouseat** **thefloor** as he wakes slowly. "What...Who? Who the fuck?" The **man** sits noticing he's **sure**, his eyes dart to me. "What's your name?" I ask circling **round** him. "What the fuck has that **were given** to do with you, you little bitch" He snarls. "Like **kids** do we?" I growl. "What's it to you? Did I take your sibling or something? I do it for the money, I **simplycirculate** them **round** that's it!" He shouts. "You take kids...Move them to **any otherarea** for them to do what with them?" I **snatch** a fist **complete** of his hair and he cries out. "I don't know! That's **now no longer** my job!" He shouts. "So you've **by no means** taken one for yourself" I say as I drop a **image** in **the front** of him. My rage is growing, and Hayden is **status** watching, **playing** the show. "I...I...I **becomesimply** getting what they owed me. They didn't pay me! So I took her! I swear it **become** a **loss of** judgement, I didn't **imply** to **harm** her!" He urges. "You **reduce** her...Beat her and left her to die **through** a river...But you didn't **imply** it?" I face him my hand spherical his large neck. "I'm sorry! I'll do anything! Don't kill me!" He cries out. "Samantha, he's already given my guys the facts we need. Dispose of him could you" Hayden says in the back of me earlier than he passes me a knife. "No!" The man screams seeking toagainfarfar from me. I take the knife and slice via his throat, blood spurting everywhere, protecting me withinside the hot, thick and sticky blood. "Mmm, my suitable blood-soaked rose" Hayden's palms come round me as his fingers play with my framebeneathneath my blouse and the blood. "Make an oath now no longerto headclose to my own circle of relatives and I'm yours. I'll damage any fucker like this. No one touches my own circle of relatives" I say as he turns me, pushing me toward the wall. "You're mine, no person will mess together along with yourown circle of relatives" He repeats earlier than taking my lips in his. I attemptnow no longer to gag, repulsed that he's touching me. But what desire did I actually have? "Happy birthday Samantha" He smirks taking my hand and main me to his office. Next Ch

Chapter Ten

I became with Hayden for an entire12 months and he had me do challenge upon challenge. I'd torn asideguys, tortured humans and finishedthe entirety he'd requested of me. Some of his personalguyschecked out me with surprise as they watched, howevera few, like Marcus, nonetheless didn't believe me. Why could they? I became the chief of the Midnight Rose they knew I desired Hayden lifeless and but I hadn't touched him. He touched me...On a day by day basis, I felt unwelleach day from it however learnt to simply take it. My thoughts had long past so inside itself I didn't recognize who I became anymore, I simply did as I becameinstructed and were given on with it with out question. I'd given up looking tobreak out, I'd attemptedearlier than and that nearlyfee me a existence of a person in my own circle of relatives. He'd come withinside the day when Iattempted to break out with picturegraph's of James crushed to a bloody pulp withinside the hospital. "What the fuck!" I screamed at Hayden as he smirked. "I warned you. You are mine. If you try andbreak outover again I can have my guys kill a personsubsequent time. This is your **best** warning" Hayden had **statedearlier than** slamming the door at the back of me as Marcus grinned, bruises on his knuckles. "You did it, didn't you?" I growled and he **simply** laughed and left. From then on I **stored** to doing as I **becameinstructed**. I behaved, I did my activity and **startedto hang around** with a number of the men. "Did **you spot** Samantha tear that **men** ear from his head!?" Seb exclaimed as we **were givenreturned** from a activity. I **becameblanketed** in blood as Hayden appreciated it. He **regularly** ordered me to live like it. "Nothing sexier than a **female** who can **manage** herself" Greyson winked and nudged me playfully. "Be **cautious** or I'll **grow to bemanaging** you" I smirk. "Damn **lady**..." He groans lustfully as I laugh. "You haven't **were given** a chance" Seb laughs, **understanding** they weren't allowed **to the touch** me. I **became** Hayden's. "Where the hell is Marcus? He's been **long past** a month now" Kai stated as he marched **via** the door. "Hopefully lifeless" I **statedbecause themen** snickered. They knew Marcus and I **desired** to kill **everydifferent** and if it wasn't for Hayden, I'm **certainthat could** have **took place** already. "Play **properly**

Samantha" Seb smirked. "Where's the amusing in being best? I gave up being best the day I were givenright here" I stated stabbing my meals with my fork. "I'm certaina part of you continues to bebest...Just a bit act isn't it" Seb replies. "We all act Seb, a few are simplyhigher than others. Or are you telling me that Hayden doesn't have some thing on all of you" I improve a forehead and all of themappearance away. Of route, Hayden didn't have followers, he used threats towardshouseholds and money owed he became owed. "Be cautious or you'll get us all killed Samantha" Greyson sighed. "I don't care anymore Greyson, allow me die" I sigh and arise throwing away my mealsearlier than leaving the room. "Samantha, my workplace please earlier than you wash up" Hayden catches me as I strollbeyond his workplace. Here we move again, any otherspherical of blood-soaked intercourse with Hayden. "What can I do for you boss?" I requested as I sat withinside the chair subsequent to his desk. "I simplydesiredto peerin case youhad been excited in your birthday tomorrow?" He smiles strollingas much as me as he choices me up and locations me on his lap, making me straddle him.

"Twenty-six...Oh joy...What you getting me?" I ask, kissing his neck like I knew he appreciated. The faster I were given this finished, the faster I ought to scold my frame of blood withinside thebathe. "A little amusing, you'll see my little blood-soaked rose" He smirks as he tears my blouse from me and starts offevolved licking the blood from my frame as I attemptnow no longer to gag. "I'm simply blood-soaked" I say as he growls lustfully earlier than pushing me to the floor, ripping my trousers away earlier than plunging himself into me. "We'll have little toddlersquickly you'll have my kids and we'll be the maximumeffective mafia withinside the world" He smirks as he maintains to thrust into me tough as I faux to moan. "I ideaown circle of relatives makes you weak" I smirk. "My own circle of relatives will now no longer be weak. We will kill who wishes to be killed, I will do thataccurate this time. They will now no longer be like my failure of a daughter. They'll be effectivesuch as you and me" He grunts as he finishes interior me, kissing my breast earlier than chucking me a blouse of his personal to cowl up. He didn't just like theguys gawping at my frame. I became his to have a take a observe, his to the touch, no person else's. "Boss!" Marcus's voice boomed as he knocked and stormed into the room. His eyes darted over my frame as I speedypositioned the blouse on. "How dare you inputwith out permission!" Hayden yells and punches Marcus withinside the jaw as I listen a crunch and his yell. "Sorry sir" He murmurs keeping his jaw. "I'll be going" I stated as I rush out the room after quacking setting my trousers returned on. I be aware Marcus have a take a observe me weirdly, now no longer his traditional scowl as I left the room. "Hey Samantha. Hayden wishes you on responsibilitywithinside the cells tonight" Seb calls at my door as I pop out of the bathe. Oh great, mobileularresponsibility, in different words, torture a person all night time as they scream for assist and I get blanketed in blood...again. "Fine" I groan as I get wearing a simple black leggings and t-blouse. "You'll like this one" Seb laughs as we head to the cells. "Will I?" I ask sarcastically. "Child killer" He smirks as he should have visible the extrade in my eyes, they knew I hated whatever to do with children being harm. "Maybe I will like it" I smirk as he chucks a knuckle duster at me and leaves me on the door with a wink. That night time I tear the fellow to portions as I get data out of him. After locating out all I ought to I beat the fellowinside an inch of his existence as he crawled at thefloorfarfar from me. "Please don't! No extra!" He cries as I take a seat downat thefloortowards the wall, blanketed in blood again. "You'll bleed out quickly enough" I stated as he simply sobbed towards the wall. Soon enough, he did simply that, slowly he started to waftfarfar from blood loss as I watched the milddepart his eyes. Then, I fell asleep sat up towards the wall. "Wakey, wakey Samantha" Greyson laughed shaking me wide consciousthe subsequent morning. "God rattling it, did I actuallydoze off in blood?" I growl on the sticky play around me. "Oh yeah, it looks as if you had your length and it exploded anywhere in right here" He laughs and drags me up, chucking a towel at me and a brand new pair of trousers. He turns and we could me extrade my trousers earlier than we depart the room. "Don't trouble going on your room. Boss wishes you withinside theworkplace" He says as I sigh in frustration. "Seriously...I simplyneed to bathe and visit bed" I groan. "Good good fortune with that nowadays birthday lady, satisfied birthday" He bows as he leaves me on theworkplace door. "Wow were givena bit blood there, babe" Seb smirks from interior gesturing my completeframe. "Be you subsequentin case you're now no longercautious" I snap and Hayden laughs. "Now, now, do play properly. It's Samantha's birthday after all" "Boss, we were given the location!" Marcus comes jogging in, unexpectedlypreventing with a glare at me. "Well do inform. Samantha can bebecoming a member of you in this one, so would possibly as properlyallow us to all recognize" Hayden "No manner is she coming! I've been operatingin this for months! He's my kill!" Marcus growls. "Looks such as yousimply went down a peg" I smirk as he steps towards me threateningly. "I'm now no longer afraid to take you out, regardless of what HE says" "Marcus...Do I want to remind you approximately your spouse and infant" Hayden growls as my eyes flick among them. "No sir. Sorry" He says as his eyes visit the floor. Did Hayden have his own circle of relatives on him too? Was he the use ofa majority of thesehumansvia way of means of threatening cherished ones.

"Good, now provide an explanation for the state of affairs to Samantha so she willmovebathe and be a part of you for extra birthday amusing" Hayden urges. "Birthday..." Marcus faces me. "Get on with it" I growl, and he snaps out of his personal thoughts. "We've been retainingan eye fixed on a small gang somecities over from right here, they've been pushing their barriers and recently have come into our town, taking our commercial enterprise. We've misplaced 50% of drug income and they've taken down as a minimum5 of our men. We controlledto seize one recently and he's squealing like a pig" Marcus's eye glint whilst he says approximatelythe fellow squealing, I becamequitecertain this manwere given off on torture...But some thingnonetheless felt...Off approximately him. "So, what's the plan?" I ask. "We tear them down. Wipe out the complete lot. Watch them burn" Marcus smirks bringing out a lighter and flicking it on menacingly. "Make certain it's bloody" Hayden's eyes glinted as he checked out me, nonethelessblanketed in blood. "That's why you need me to head..." I nod. "Of route my little blood-soaked rose. We ought to make a statement, what higher than you to head and wreck them...In fact, don't bathe, live in those." He smirks as I grimace. "I am now no longer ruining my vehicle" Marcus snarls. "Take the van" Seb says casually. "You're severely making me exiton this?" I ask. "Yes. Have amusing. Now get out" Hayden smirks earlier than shooing us off. "If you try and run, I'll shoot you myself" Marcus growls as he leads us down the corridor. "I actually havean excessive amount of to lose" I sigh as I be aware his eyes flicker to mine earlier than going returned to his evil glare. "Here, take these" He says as we get to a room packed with weapons, handing me somelengthy knives. "Don't I get a gun too?" I ask pointing to the only he became loading. "Not a chance" He laughs and drags me out of the room. "Hold up! It's simply us going?" I forestallunexpectedly as he receives into the van. "Scared sweetheart?" He increases a forehead as I frown and leap in. "How many humanscan be in there?" I ask as he starts offevolved driving. "Fifteen maybe" He shrugs. "Fifteen to two...that sounds fair..." He huffs and takes out his 2d gun, handing it to me. "If you pull that on me..." He growls out. "Hayden has an excessive amount of on me for that" I sigh as he nods, and we take a seat down in silence. What the hell became I doing? I ought to shoot this man and force off! But Hayden had guys on my own circle of relatives, it became like I became stuck! I had no conceptwherein we had been and didn't recognizewhatever as we drove via streets earlier thansooner or later pulling to a forestallwherein Marcus introduced out a big duffel bag, unzipping it as I noticed the make-shift explosives. "Which constructing?" I ask, even though there weren't many as we sat in an business estate, it became quiet, commercial enterprise hours weren't on us but, the solarslightlygrowingwithinside the sky. "The one up ahead" He says as I be aware it's a vehicleelements warehouse. "Lots of locationsto cover in an area like that" I say. "Yep" is all he says. "This is ridiculous, we're going to die" I say as we get out the van and flowspeedy, if all peoplenoticed the blood on me they'd name the police. "Shut up and get on" He growls as we get to the the front, we creep across thefacet of the constructingseeking out a manner in as I listen shouts come from interior. "Did you listen that the Midnight Rose ladywere given taken? Pretty certain she's lifelessvia way of means of now" I heard one say because it piqued my interest. "No mannerguy, Hayden's were given her locked up somewhere. There's a bounty out to discover her. Man...If best, we'd be finished with all this" Another voice stated as I observeda grin on Marcus's face. "In you move. Get their believe, that's our manner to do that" He smirks "You're joking...Putting me instantlywithinside thecenter of them!" I whisper, shout. "Can you observed of a highermanner?" He snaps as I sigh. "Fine" I answer. "Do play the part. We've simply escaped from Hayden and wantassist" He says locking me into his facet with a smirk, his hand withinside the blood as he smears a few on himself to make it appear to be we'd escaped, howeverslightly. "Hey! Hey! Help me!" I cry out as I bang towards the door as Marcus starts offevolved pretending to observe our backs. "What the fuck?" a personsolutions as his eyes widen. "Please you need toassist us!" I cry as we push our manner in. "Who are you? What took place to you?" He pulls out a gun. "Please! Don't! I simplyneed to get to my own circle of relatives!" I cry out as my eyes dart across the room. "What's your name?" any other asks as humansstart flooding into the room. "Samantha...Samantha Jones" I say, and I listen them gasp. "You're the middle of the night rose lady!" One exclaims. "Will you cover us? Please, simplyallow us to lay low" Marcus asks. "Who are you boy?" A hugeguy comes out from a door in the front as he appears over the pair of us. "He became locked up with me, please, we wantassist" I say as I matteras a minimum twelve menround us. "Come right here" The bigman beckons me forwards. "Not with out me" Marcus growls. "What will you do boy? You're outnumbered." He laughs. "I don't see many guns, simply this one and you" He nods closer tothe fellow who becameon the door. "We don't address guns, now no longer our thing..." He says. "That's a shame..." Marcus smirks and movements off of me because the destruction starts offevolved. Marcus takes out the hugemanspeedy as I shoot closer tothe fellowon the door. "Watch it!" Marcus shouts as any otherguy comes from at the back of me, I knock my head backwards as I listen a crunch. One via way of means of one we take them down as we depart a bloodied pathanywhere. "Check down there, I'll end off up right here" Marcus orders as I head for the door wherein the hugeman, who I became guessing became the chiefgot here from. "Don't...Please..." He's now no longerlifeless! He grabs keep of my trousers. "I..." I start as I listenmotion downstairs, the personwe couldmove as he dies from blood loss. I stroll slowly down the steps with my gun raised. "Daddy! What became that huge bang?!" A little ladyinvolvesthe lowest of the stepsand appears at me with horror. She screams and runs off as I run down the steps. "Don't harm us" A female cries because the little lady hides at the back of her. "Is it clean?!" Marcus calls out. "Please..." The female cries. "Hide...Find the Midnight Rose, inform them Samantha despatched you" I say speedy as they speedyflowright into acabinet. "It's clean down right here" I shout as I start my manner up. "You checked properly?" He increases a forehead and pushes beyond me. "Seriously, you're checking my work! There's no person down right here!" I shout as he starts offevolved kicking down desks. I listen a whimper as he kicks any other and desire he didn't listen it. "What became that?" He swirls round. "What?" I ask. "I heard some thing" He says as he opens the cabinet and grabs the female and her infant out via way of means of their hair as they scream. "It's only a kid!" I shout as he pushes me away and makes them kneel in the front of him. "You lied…You knew they had been there didn't you?" He says searching from me to them. "Please, allow us tomove!" The female cries. "How the hell are humans going to discover what took placeright here if we kill every person? You ever consider that?!" I ask as his nostrils flare in anger. "We had beenprepurported to kill every person! You disobeyed!" He shouts pointing a gun at me. "Shoot me I dare you. People will discoverapproximately this if we depart them alive" I say stepping in the front of him. "We'll see what Hayden has to mention shall we?" He says with a cocky smirk as he receives out his telecellsmartphone and places it on loud speaker. "Is it finished?" Hayden calls out, now no longer bothering with pleasantries. "Not quite, we've had a bit hiccup together along with your rose" He says. "Oh?" "She concealed up a bitlady and her mother. She attempted to keep them." Marcus says because thetelecellsmartphone is silent. "I bestsupposed it as a manner to unfoldphrase, if every person dies on this then how will phraseunfold that you, Hayden, have me as an accomplice. That you've got got me operating for you, taking down your personal enemies" I say in desire that I hadn't fucked up. "Well, that may be a very smart notion...However, I trust that becamenow no longer what I requested to be finished. Kill the female, departthe kid" He says as Marcus receives out his gun and shoots the female as the child screams. "Done" Marcus says as I stand in shock. "Take a picturegraph, I will ensure to ship it to the complete of Midnight Rose" Hayden says earlier thanplacing up. Marcus brings up his digital digicam and takes a picturegraph in the front of the kid and female with my gun and knife bloodied up in my hand.

Chapter Eleven

Marcus left the little woman soaked in her mother's blood as he dragged me upstairs and out to the van earlier than racing down the streets as I sobbed. "Be happy that Hayden appears to be in a terrific mood" He growls at me. "Who did I simplyactually kill?" I ask. "Competition" Is all he stated. "Was it actually?" I snap. "They mighthad been...eventually" He shrugs, and I groan in frustration. He'd taken my guns as we left and proper now I desirednot anythinggreater than to stab him. "You motherfuckers! They had beenharmless! Weren't they?!" I shout. "As harmless as a baby" he smirks as I smack his arm hard, he veers off pathearlier than straightening again up whilst aiming his gun at me. "You'll pay for that" He sneers. When we get again he drags me out of the van via way of means of the hair as I scream out in pain. "What the bloody hell do you watched you're doing Marcus?" Hayden growls coming to peer what became going on. "She hit me!" He snaps. "You don't appearance beaten...Can't had been that bad" Hayden pushes Marcus to the wall. "She's now no longer what she seems, she'll fuck us over" Marcus attempts to persuade. "I made it apparent I hate you all. I'm now no longer doing this for pleasure!" I growl as Hayden laughs. "She is aware of she's mine Marcus. Can't you managea bitwoman like her?" "She'll get us all killed" He says as Hayden shoves him away. "I could bedisplaying her this night why she can not do that. I deliberatesome other little surprise...Go wash up, placed on the outfit at themattress Samantha, we're going to a party" he seems over my frame biting his lip on the blood. "What party?" I ask. "You'll see" He stated shooing me away. What became he gambling at? Why might he take me to a party?

Chapter Twelve

I got in my room and saw the outfit he wanted me in, it was a sleek black dress, the skirt was leather as the torso was corset like, it went to the floor with a masquerade mask.

"Not again" I murmur as I slowly walk to the shower and scold myself with the water as the blood drips down the drain.

I put on the dress as a woman comes in and claims she was there to do my hair and make-up. She curls my hair and gives me an over the top smoky look as she places the mask on my face.

When we are finished she leads me to Hayden's office.

"My, what a wonder...You truly are a beautiful woman. Are you ready for some fun? I'm afraid we'll be blindfolding you on the way there, can't have you knowing where we are going can we?" He smirks as Seb comes up with a blindfold and covers my eyes.

"Try not to ruin her hair!" The woman cries out as Hayden laughs.

Someone takes my arm as I lift my dress, so I don't trip on it.

I'm placed into a vehicle and hear the engine roar to life.

"There are rules tonight. One, you may not talk to anyone. Two, you may choose one person to dance with and that is it. Three, give us away and my men will shoot. Understood?" He says.

"Understood" I answer but I have no idea what's going on.

We ride in the car for what feels like hours before he stops the car and comes around to my side before taking my hand and removing the blindfold.

"No..." I murmur in shock as I notice where we are.

"Yes, this is your little school. Happy birthday. Tonight I will be sending that photo and many others of your work as you will watch them all receive it. They'll think you've turned with all the rumours I've put out. Remember my rules Samantha, I wouldn't want my men to hurt anyone. Notice the ones with small black roses in their pockets...They're mine...There's at least ten here. One word and I will order them to shoot." He says in my ear as he leads me to the doors.

We entered the school as my heart was beating fast, why did they do masks again? Why after Henderson's school?

We wandered around the room for a while as Hayden said hello to the men with black roses.

The hall went quiet as someone walked on the huge stage that had been put up in the hall. It looked gorgeous in here.

"Welcome! Welcome to the Academy of the Rose, thank you for celebrating the birthday of our little lady Louisa. We also wish to celebrate the birthday of our girl Samantha, although she's not here, she is never forgotten" Tobias stood on a stage in front of everyone.

"Happy Birthday Samantha!" I hear James shout as I look towards where he was, he was clapping and hollering with a smile as some others join in. I tried to stop the tear in my eye from falling.

"Now, we want to thank all of you attending as we know many of you have been helping us on our search for our girl. So, please enjoy yourself as tomorrow we'll be back to business!" He says as everyone claps.

"Very cute" Hayden laughs as he takes my hand and twirls me around on the dance floor.

"Why would you do this?" I ask.

"You earnt it. I give rewards and today you earnt a reward. Do you know who you'll dance with yet?" He smirks twirling me again as I look around.

Men were stationed across the hall as I noticed the roses on their pockets, some red and some black.

My eyes scan the room as they zero in on my grandfather who looks solemn, my heart bled as I saw Lindsey try to cheer him up and Tobias boom up to him.

"I've chosen" I say as Hayden smiles and releases my hand.

"Remember, no talking" He says releasing me as I walk through the crowd up towards them.

How the hell was I supposed to ask someone to dance if I couldn't talk?

Luckily for me as I walked up I noticed him stand and take Lindsey to the dance floor. If anyone was going to know it was me without it talking, he'd be the one, but I had to warn him somehow about the men surrounding me. I sighed as Hayden lurked in the crowd around me, watching.

"Are you ok Miss?" Tobias walked up to me with a brow raised. I just nod and he frowns as I watch the people around me.

"Not much of a talker, huh?" He says as my eyes flick to his, shaking my head a little.

"Do me a favour sweetheart...Blink once
for yes and twice for no" He says quietly
so I'm the only one who hears him.
"Do you know who I am?"
Blink once. Yes.
"Do I know you?" Tobias don't do this...
Blink once. Yes.
"Are we in danger?"
Blink once. Yes.
"Is Hayden here?" My eyes flick to his
before I blink once.
"Sam?" He gasps.
I blink once.
"We'll get you home I swear"
I blink twice as I smile at him and shake
my head, laying a hand on his arm as if
denying him a dance as Hayden watches
me carefully.
"Sorry, is my date bothering you?"
Hayden comes up quickly.
"Oh, no, if anything I was. She wouldn't
say a word to me, I only asked for a
dance" Tobias says eyeing up Hayden.
"Well, I am sorry, she's mute. Had her
tongue cut out when she was younger" He
said but I could hear the warning in his
voice.
"That's awful. Sorry to hear that. Now, if
you'll excuse me, I have to mingle. I

apologise for bothering you Miss" He says with a bow and kisses my hand.

"What are you playing at?" Hayden hisses in my ear as he drags me to the dance floor once more, pulling me close to him.

"He was asking for a dance. I didn't say anything. I was waiting for a moment to try and get a dance with the person I wanted, but he's dancing, and I'm not allowed to talk" I hiss.

"Fine, show me who and I'll swap you out for whomever they are dancing with"

I looked around and didn't see grandpa anywhere anymore.

"Shit, they've gone" I growl.

"Then choose another, before I lose my patience" He snaps as I look around as I point to someone.

But before we can get to them Hayden is tapped on the shoulder.

"Do you mind if I dance with the lovely lady here?" The person asks.

"I'm not sure if my date would like to. Would you like to my love?" He asks as I look at the man, I couldn't work out who it was.

"Please?" The guy begs.

"Fine. But we leave soon, so make it quick" Hayden huffs, choosing for me and passes my hand to the man as he twirls me around.

I notice Tobias and a few others crowd around us as Hayden is hidden from sight.

"I know it's you Sam. Tobias told us. Same rules as him, I know you're scared. Blink once for yes, two for no." He says.

I blink once. I still can't work out who it is...I hate these masks!

"Do you know who I am?" They ask as I have to stop myself laughing, I didn't have a clue, I blink twice.

"These masks work well...It's me, Zane" He says as my eyes widen, but I lower them quickly.

"He has men here doesn't he? Watching us?"

I blink once, yes.

"How many?" He asks as he twirls me slowly around as I count.

I blink slowly ten times.

"Ten...Shit...you know which ones?" He asks.

Blink once, yes.

"So their outfit is different?"

Yes.

"It's the roses isn't it?" He says as I smile lightly and blink once.

Suddenly the hall is filled with ring tones and the dancing stops.

"Black roses?" He asks as I blink once. He nods as he opens his phone up and gazes at the screen.

Screams fill the room and the room is filled with loud conversation.

"Tell me you didn't..." He says as he shows me the screen.

It showed an image.

"Your girl isn't so innocent is she? These men were innocent, they were much like you, protecting the children, an ally of the Midnight Rose. Looks like she's mine forever!" The message said as it showed every bloodied body and then a photo of the little girl on the ground, dead, it had been edited like I was looking at her like a trophy

The whole room was in uproar as people rushed about talking about the message.

"I'll take her back now, thank you" Hayden said coming up to me.

Suddenly Hayden's leg was rammed into as he tumbled to the ground.

"What the hell?!" He shouts as I spot it was Shaun in the wheelchair.

"Oh my! I'm sorry, I'm not used to the chair yet! Paralysed, my man. I apologise. Are you ok miss?" He says as his hand takes a hold of my dress slightly as he places a pin on it.

I nod as Hayden growls in annoyance.

"Let's go!" Hayden shouts waiting for me.

"Ladies and gentlemen! Can I have your attention for just a moment?" Tobias booms as Hayden pulls me to his side as everyone stops and faces the stage once more.

"It has come to my attention that an image and message has been sent to all regarding our girl Samantha. May I remind you that all roses have thorns, and this one is a very black rose indeed! Do not forget that there is always more sides to a story! Unfortunately, you are all being misled! Samantha has been taken and used against her will" He continues.

"Let's go" Hayden growls and slowly drags me away from the crowd. But it wasn't unnoticed.

"Oh don't leave sir! The party just started!" Tobias booms out as the doors behind us close.

"What are you playing at man? A lock in?" Hayden tries to laugh.

"Of sorts...I'm asking everyone to remove their masks. In our lifetime we all put on a mask and tonight we put a stop to that. We want to show our true faces." He smirks.

Tobias no! I wish I could convey this to him. This was not going to end well.

"We do however have to do one thing first..." My grandpa took the stage.

I looked to my dress as I saw the pin. If they were about to do something, that would be my only weapon.

"Boys!" Tobias booms as shots ring in the air as the men with black roses on their suits go down one by one.

"God damn it! What did you do!" Hayden hissed in my ear as I felt him searching for his gun.

"Looking for something?" Shaun wheeled up to us twirling a gun in his hand with a smirk.

But before I knew it a blade was up to my throat.

"Missed this though didn't you boy?" Hayden laugh.

"Put the knife down" A voice says from behind us as he twirls us around to face Lizzy with a gun.

"Darling! How are you? I've been looking for you!" He says.

"Oh really? Looking for me why? Because I thought I was too weak for you" She says.

"Just a joke baby girl." He says as he presses the knife harder to my throat as I whimper.

"Get your hands off my girl" This time we whirl to Jayden standing there, his mask off now too.

"Jay" I cry.

"Or what? I'll take her with me if you try to kill me. Then what will you have?" He says as my hand slowly inches up the skirt of my dress to the pin.

"You aren't getting out of here Hayden" I say.

"Neither will you, not without a box" He laughs.

"I warned you my family were stronger, didn't I?" I said.

"The boys will come after you, if you kill me, they'll still come after you. I'm sure Marcus will love to drain blood from every one of you!" He shouts.

"Will I?" I hear as Marcus comes out of the crowd.

"About time you got here" Lizzy smiles.

"What?!" Hayden and I say at the same time, this gives me the leverage to grab the knife at my throat, stab his hand with the pin as he shouts in pain as Lizzy wipes out her father's legs.

"Shaun might have taught me your move"
Lizzy smirks, her gun still zeroed in on
her father.

"Samantha..." Marcus says as he brings
out the little girl from the industrial
estate.

"You didn't kill her?" I murmur.

"Whole thing was a set up. They're all
alive..." He says with a smile as the guys I
thought we'd killed came out of the
crowd.

"Daddy, you've pissed off a lot of people
here. Any final words?" Lizzy says.

"Fuck you" He says.

"Lizzy give me the gun" I say as she goes
to shoot.

She walks around her father and hands
me the gun as I remove my own mask.

"You broke me down, drowned me,
tortured me, had your men play with me
and then thought you had me...I warned
you my family were stronger, and it looks
like even your own men wanted MY life.
Men like you will NEVER win...Not now,
not ever, not while we're around" I growl
as I kick his knife away as he looks at me
with fear.

"Well played...Your mother would be
proud...I'll be sure to tell her everything
you've done when I'm up there with her.

It will be great to see her again if you know what I mean" he winks as I growl and get closer.

"You'll be in hell nowhere near her" I say as he smirks.

Within a few seconds he's grabbed the gun from my hands, pulled my legs from under me and is aiming at me from the edge of the hallway.

"You should have just got on with it!" He laughs.

The doors open behind him as his smile faulters.

"Stay away from my Aunty!" Layla screams out as I notice a gun in her hand as she pulls the trigger.

Hayden falls to the ground with a thud as we look at the scene wide-eyed in shock.

"LAYLA!" Tammy, Wayne and Rob shout as they run up to her tear-stricken face.

Hayden was still breathing on the ground as I ignored everything going on around me kicking his gun away and dragging him outside with the knife in my hand.

"Damn kids" He coughed up blood.

"Sam…" Tobias says from the doorway.

"Enjoy hell fucker, say hey to the men that wrecked my life" I said before slowly slitting his throat as he gurgles out, blood all over me once more.

"Sammy" Tobias says again from the door.

"Who gave Layla a fucking gun?" I scowl.

"We'll find out where she got it...Sam are you ok?" He asks as I walk back into the building with blood over my arms.

"Oh no! Aunty Sammy! Did you get hurt?!" Layla screams running to me.

"I'm ok, it's not my blood Layla baby" I said with a smile.

"I...I didn't mean to shoot him...He was going to hurt you...Cody needs his mummy I need my aunty...We missed you" She bowed her head.

"Layla, I'm not happy about you using a gun, not at your age. But thank you" My voice wobbled in the end.

"Kitten!" Jayden runs up to me, ignoring the blood on me as he kisses me hard on the lips as I completely lose it and begin to sob.

"I'm home..." I cry.

"You're home. We've got you" He says trying to soothe me as I drop to the floor.

"I want this place tidied up! Nights not over yet and the party just started! We got our girl home!" Tobias boomed from the stage as many of the men began clearing up the bodies on the ground.

"Jay, let me take her, I'll get her cleaned up" Savannah comes to my side as she helps me up and steers me upstairs.

"Cody?" I ask, still blubbing.

"Under the watch of Uncle Damien and Uncle Taylor" She says.

"Taylor's ok?" I ask.

"He's got some major scarring, but he's ok" She says as she helps me out of the blood-soaked dress and into one of the showers.

"Marcus was in on this?" I say once out of the shower as she sits me down with a huge towel wrapped around me.

"He wasn't...not to begin with... But then Harvey and Tobias got to him...We've not stopped looking for you Sam" She says as she hugs me tight to her side.

"I was lost myself...I was breaking..." I cry.

"But you didn't, you're home. It's over" She kisses my head.

"Happy birthday to me" I laugh as she chuckles too and helps me into another dress.

"I bought this for you for your birthday...I hope you like it" She says as I look in the mirror. It was beautiful. A gorgeous red dress that hugged my figure. I'd lost a little weight thanks to Hayden's starvation techniques, but it still looked great.

"Thank you"

"We thought you were dead…" She cried suddenly as I wrapped my arms around her.

"I'm here" I murmured.

"He sent us messages, photos of you, of what he did…Then he sent one, you looked dead…We didn't want to believe it…Tobias point blank refused to let us as he and the guys kept digging. They found Marcus. They got his family to safety and he agreed to help…Hayden's been using families as a way of control for so long that his men have forgotten…Tobias persuaded him…If it wasn't for him…" She sniffled.

"Tobias was the one who recognised me tonight…" I said as she nodded.

"He came straight to find us when he'd figured out you were really here" She smiled.

"I owe him so much" I cried.

"Then we need to stop crying and get ourselves together as he wants to party" She laughs a little as I chuckle and hug her tightly once more.

"Thank you for taking care of Cody" I said as she smiled.

"How did you know?" She asks.
"Hayden threatened me with a video call of you all up the park...The day I gave in to the torture" I said.
"Well you don't need to worry about that anymore. Cody misses his mummy we'll see him soon" she smiles and takes my hand, leading me back downstairs.
The hall was already back to the image of joy it had been before, the bodies and masks gone.
As we come into the hall it erupts into applause as I go bright red blushing.
"Happy Birthday Samantha and Louisa!"
The crowd cheer as I cry with happiness.

Chapter Thirteen

I run up to the stage where Tobias is stood with a huge smile at me as I jump up into his arms.

"Thank you" I cry as he booms with laughter.

"Savannah told you, huh? You don't need to thank me. I knew you were alive I could feel it" He says kissing my head.

"How'd you know it was me?" I said pointing to the spot where he had noticed me.

"I was watching the crowd and noticed a pretty girl, I noticed the scar on your chest from being shot, I don't know how Hayden didn't pick up on that one... But most of all, I noticed how much you looked like your mother tonight. Hayden made the mistake of putting you in a dress similar to the one your mother once wore to a gala" He says as we make our way down to the dance floor.

"Thank you again Tobias. May I have this dance?" I ask as he laughs and takes my hand, twirling me before I'm caught by another pair of arms.

"I'm not the man you should be dancing with right now" He laughs and walks away.

"Kitten...You look beautiful...I missed you" He said kissing my lips.

"I missed you too. I love you" I smiled as he took my lips again with passion as he lifted me up and twirled us as I laughed.

"This feels so crazy, we had all this planned for last year as a surprise party and I had a huge surprise for you. But then everything happened, and I didn't think I'd ever get the chance to do this..." He says as I look at him frowning in confusion.

"A chance to do what?" I ask as he gets down on one knee and brings out a small red ring box.

The whole hall goes quiet as everyone watches.

"Mummy!" I hear Cody scream as his little legs barrel him into me as I swing him around as the crowd awes. He looked so big, he'd grown so much this past year, I'd missed my baby so much.

"Little busy here buddy" Jayden laughs.

"Sorry daddy" Cody smiles but doesn't let go.

"Samantha Jones, we weren't sure if we would get you back and tonight was a luck of the draw if you turned up or not. I think you are the bravest woman I have ever known. You defeat all odds and keep coming home to us, even when the stakes get tougher and I think…I think you won't come back to us. I love you so much and you've given me a family I will never forget. I love you and I love Cody as if he's my own. So, after the events of tonight especially, will you do me the honour of marrying me?" He asks as the crowd goes silent.

"Say yes mummy" Cody says in my ear.

The crowd chuckles again.

"Cody thinks I should say yes… You said once I was a pain in your ass…You sure you still want me?" I smirk.

"Kitten, you're killing me here, of course I want you. I want everything that involves you. I love you" He says standing, pushing a strand of hair from my face.

"Come here buddy" Savannah grabs Cody from my arms quickly.

"Yes" I smile as Jayden jumps and fist pumps the air before taking the ring and placing it on my finger as I look at it. It's a beautiful red rose gem.

"I love you Kitten" He kisses me and swings me around.

The whole crowd goes wild with cheering.

"Get off Aunt Sav!" Cody shouts as he escapes her clutches and jumps into my arms as I kiss his head.

"I love you so much baby boy" I cry.

"Mummy no sad" He frowns.

"I'm not sad, they are happy tears baby" I smile as Jayden kisses both our heads.

"Sammy?"

I turn to the voice as I see Taylor and Damien slowly walking their way towards us.

"Taylor!" I cry out.

"Be careful! He's under strict instruction to not over do it! He's still healing! He's had some of the scar tissue operated on." Damien says quickly.

"You fucking flatlined arsehole!" I smirked at him with a tear in my eye, I hadn't forgotten that day.

"Pay back is a bitch" He says with a wince.

"Fucking idiot. I love you Taylor" I said carefully hugging him as he tugged me to him as I felt him wince.

"Couldn't let you do this without me could I?" He smiles.

"I'm so glad you'll be ok. I was so scared" I cry, my hands shaking against his.

"We all were, it got even worse when you disappeared" Damien said.

I spot Marcus in the distance with the guys from the industrial estate.

"Excuse me a minute" I put up a finger and storm up to him, slapping him in the face as it rings out through the hall.

"Sammy!" Savannah shouts in shock, running to me.

"Don't...I deserved that...And more" He says running a hand over where I slapped him.

"You couldn't have just warned me...Told me something...Anything!" I shout.

"How was I supposed to do that? He was watching us like a hawk!" He says back.

"How about before we went in and I thought I killed them!" I point to the guys behind as I notice the big guy come forward with the little girl.

"We knew the danger...Some of my men were hurt, but they all made it. You don't need to worry about us Miss Jones" He says.

"Your wife?" I ask.

"Is at home" he smiles as I let out a breath.

"How?" I ask

"Your bullets were blood pellets and the knife was blunt as hell, you couldn't cut anything with that" Marcus laughs.

"How the hell did I not notice..." I murmur.

"Hayden had your mind completely, so you forgot details of your weapons as they weren't the priority" Marcus sighed.
"Your family are safe?"
"Yes. Thanks to your men" He nods.
"Then go. Go home. Don't come back, stay out of this life" I said, and he looks at me in shock.
"But..." He says
"We'll sort you money and a new place, go be with your family. All of you too" I nodded to the people behind.
"That's kind of you ma'am" They nod and begin to walk out.
"Thank you..." Marcus nods and rushes outside to his car.
"We'll sort them out" Luka comes to my side as I see him for the first time tonight.
"Luka!" I said and jumped into my brother's arms.
"You're doing that a lot tonight" He laughed but hugged me tightly.
"Can you blame her?" James laughed from his side as I hugged him too.
"I missed you guys" I said as my legs were taken out from beneath me and I landed on a lap.
"This chair thing is fun" Shaun says as his arms wrap around me.

"You're enjoying it too much" Elise says kissing my cheek.

"Do you guys mind giving me my future wife back please?" Jayden walked up with Cody in his arms, beaming.

"Yeah! Give mummy back!" Cody points at them sternly.

I got off Shaun's lap and went up to my two boys as they cuddled me tightly with a smile.

My head was in a spin with everything going on and it was finally taking its toll as my hands began to shake.

I was suddenly lifted from the ground and carried away as I laughed.

"Grandpa! You're going to hurt yourself!" I laugh as he puts me down outside.

"Let it out" he says.

"Let what out?" I say, but he knows I'm close to breaking down.

"Samantha...this has been a crazy year...let it all out...I know you need to. You are home and happy, but you're not here completely are you?" He says as I sigh.

"It's all so...much...It's always so much..." I said before the damn opens and the tears come falling as he hugs me to him and lets me just cry it all out.

"We'll sort your head out. We will. One step at a time. I know it's not going to be easy and tonight was a lot, I told Jayden not to propose tonight if you turned up but the boy did it anyway...I see why, but it may not have been the time" Grandpa said as he stroked my hair.

"It was fine, it just took me by surprise. This whole day...it's been crazy. I don't feel like me anymore Grandpa...I've done a lot of bad things..." I sigh.

"You don't need to worry about that anymore sweetheart, not anymore..." He holds my head in his hands, tears in his eyes.

"Mummy!" Cody runs outside and jumps into my arms.

"Hi baby, you got so big!" I cry as I kiss his face all over.

"I'm nearly three! Where'd you go mummy" He frowns as I look at Grandpa.

"Cody, you know the bad man took your mummy. But she's home now. We got her back like we promised" Grandpa said.

"No one take mummy again" Cody hugs me tight.

"I'm not going anywhere baby boy" I wrap my arms around him tight, crying silently.

We make our way back inside the school as I stand in the doorway as people are dancing around once more.

"Aunty Sammy?" Layla walks slowly up to me with Tammy behind her.

"What the hell were you thinking Layla?" I said as she bowed her head.

"I just...I just wanted you home...Wanted to keep you safe, I heard Tobias from upstairs and found the gun in your old desk...I wanted to keep you safe" She said as I knelt down. She'd grown too, almost eleven years old now.

"Thank you. But no more guns ok? Promise me" I said as a tear escaped as I placed a finger under her chin and lifted her face to mine.

"I promise." She cries before hugging me tight as I look at Tammy as she holds my hand with tears in her eyes. It would be an emotional night.

"Cody, can I have mummy for a little while?" Taylor walks up to me as Cody nods and runs to Jayden as they both watch me with a smile.

"Where are we going?" I ask as he takes my hand and leads me away from the hustle and bustle of the room, into my old office.

"You've lost your shine. I've been watching you the whole night since we found out it was you. You're not really here are you? Not in your mind" He says holding my hand tightly in his as we sit together on the sofa.

I look at the scars on his hands and arms, reminding me of the day I almost lost him.

"I don't know Taylor...It's been a year, I missed you all, I really did. But...I feel...dead inside" I sighed and placed my head on his shoulder carefully.

"What did he do to you?" he sighs.

"What didn't he do..." I said as I began to tell him everything, I needed the release and he just let me talk as I told him everything.

By the end of it his eyes were fogged up with tears.

"Taylor, how do I live with it? How he touched me? All those memories. Plus, I think...I think...I think I might be pregnant..." I sob as he looks at me in shock.

"You've got to be kidding...Shit Sam" He cries out and hugs me.

"How could Jayden ever still love me when he finds out?" I cry.

"That guy will love you no matter what. We all do. We'll get through this. Hayden

is dead, you never have to go back again"
He strokes my hair as I sob.

"I don't know if I want it...It's his...How could I look at a child knowing who it's father was?" I cry, turmoil in my heart, if I was pregnant with Hayden's child, could I deal with that?

"Could you deal with getting rid of an innocent life? I know it would be his, but it's part of you too" Taylor says.

"I just don't know what to do anymore Taylor" I say.

"Just think on it first, don't be too hasty. We are all here for you" He kisses my head as I lean against him carefully.

"May I come in?" There was a knock on the door as Rueben enters the room.

"Hey Rueben" I smile.

"I thought I could give you a quick check up with Lindsey here. We just wanted to see if you're ok" They entered the room as Lindsey came up and hugged me tightly to her like a mother would her own child.

"I'm...Physically ok" I said as Rueben nodded, he knew what I meant, he knew I was in mental turmoil.

Taylor placed a kiss on my head as Lindsey quickly looked me over in the bathroom.

"A lot of scarring, but you seem ok. Any pain?" She asks.

"No" I answer.

"Shall we go home?" Lindsey says as I nod in her arms.

"Go and get Cody, he needs his mummy and I'll let Tobias and the others know you're leaving. Anyone you want to come home with you in particular?" Rueben asks.

"Taylor. I told him. I told him everything" I said as another tear escaped.

We went out front as Rueben went looking for the others.

"Mummy go home now?" Cody ran up to me with a smile as Taylor, Damien and Jayden followed close behind.

"Yeah, mummy coming home" I smile and pick him up, kissing his cheek.

"Tobias is shutting down the party soon, figured we all needed a good nights rest." Jayden walked up to me slowly, placing a kiss on my cheek as I flinched, and he frowned.

"Sorry" I said as we got to the cars.

"It's ok" He frowns and backs up a little.

"Jayden why don't you help shut down the party, we'll take Sam home and meet you there soon" Taylor says as Jayden sighs and nods.

"Love you kitten, take care of your mummy Cody" Jayden kisses Cody's head and then goes to kiss me as I flinch and he backs off, the look of hurt in his eyes killed me.

I get in the car with Taylor, Rueben, Lindsey and Cody as we drive away I see Jayden talking with Damien.

"Sammy, stop, he still loves you." Taylor says taking my hand over Cody's body as the car sends him to sleep.

"I don't know Taylor you didn't see the hurt in his eyes when he touched me. I didn't mean to flinch, but...Hayden's the only one who's touched me with kisses and other things for the past year... I just...I got scared..." I say.

"It will get better. In time. Jayden will understand" Lindsey says.

I rest my head on the cold window as we drive down the streets that I missed for a long time, but I couldn't help feeling empty inside.

Was this my life anymore, after a year of torturing and killing, could I go back to normal and be a mother like everyone expected me to be?

My hands shook the closer we got to the house.

"Sammy lets get you indoors" Rueben caught my attention as I hadn't noticed we had stopped, parked outside the house.
I slowly got out of the car as my eyes scoured the house, Lindsey took Cody from the car, asleep in her arms.
"I'll help you. Just one step at a time Sammy" Taylor links his fingers with mine as he tries to help me stop shaking.
"I can't do this..." I shake.
"Yes you can. We've got you" Rueben comes up to me and places a hand on my shoulder.

Slowly we make our mannerinterior as my eyes take withinside the house. It became a mess, snap shotshad been strewn towards the tables, snap shots of Marcus, Seb, Greyson, Kai, Hayden and me. "How did you get those?" I ask as I undergo them, recognising while the photoshad been taken. "We had a personship them to us, we nonetheless don't recognize who" Taylor says. "Who despatched you photos of the men I becamerunning with? Why?" I ask as my eyes pass over each image. "Maybe we ought togo away this for this night and speakwithinside the morning" Rueben says as Lindsey follows in the back of him with out Cody as she had placed him to mattress. "No. Who the hell took those?" I repeat. "We don't recognize. They had beendespatched to us, we haven't had some thing else, simplyphotos, there are a fewgreater in an envelope, however we don't go away them out due to the kids" Rueben says as he opens a locked cupboard and passes over an envelope. I listenautomobiles and motorcyclesinput the driveway as I draw out the photo's from the envelope and gasp. "You realize the human beings in those?" Taylor asks. "Yeah, I'm the only who did that to all of them…" I gulp as I see the destruction I had executed over the year. "I idea you had been going to mattressyounger lady" Tobias walks in with my Grandpa in the back of him, his hands crossed as he notices the photo's in my hand. "We aren't doing this this night Samantha" Grandpa says taking the record from my arms and turning me farfar from the snap shots. "I did that…" I stated as his eyes went wide. "You had been made to. It wasn't your fault that the oneshuman beings died" He says. "Do you realize who they had been?" I ask, they had beenretainingsome thing from me. "We recognizea fewrecords yes. But now no longerthis night" He shakes his head. "They had beenharmless weren't they" I stand my floor as he turns again to me from main me from the room. "Sam, it's pleasantnow no longer to delve into this this night. We'll kind it out while you've were givena few rest" Luka enters the corridor. "Who the fuck have I killed?!" I scream as all and sundryseems at me in shock. "People we'd despatched to assistdiscover you" Luka answered. "He advised me they had beena part ofintercourse rings, traffickers, ill and twisted guys…Why did I agree with his words?" My hand went to my mouth with a puff and a sob. "Sammy..." Taylor locations a hand on my shoulder as I shake it off and run from **all of them** as I bolt out the **again** door and out onto the **seaside** as I scream and fall to my knees. Scenes flicker in my head **of eachventure** we had **long gone** on **withinside the** year. Hayden had had me kill all **folks that** had gotten **nearlocating** me, he made me kill my **personal** allies and I had **executed** so painfully. I **became** a killer. "Samantha..." "Leave me alone" I cried on my knees. "You **aren't** a monster Samantha, he did this to you, he coerced you to do this. You **aren't** a murderer" Tobias sits beside me. "I fucking **loved** it..." I **appearance** to him as he nods with a sigh. "You **idea** they **had beendistinctsorts ofguys**...You did what you **ideabecameproper** with the **records**you had" He says. "Nothing however a blood-soaked rose...He did it...He broke me...Turned me into what he desired...He **cherished** it after Igot **hereagain** to him **blanketed** in blood calling me his blood-soaked rose. But it wasn't **simply** me he **supposed**, he **supposed** that I **became** killing my **personalhuman** beings this **complete** time, I killed **guys** of the Midnight Rose" "You **aren'tdamaged** Samantha. You are higher than this. You will make it via this. It's over" He says searching into my eyes. "It's in no way over...I can't forestall this urge to needto teara person's throat out, to smashthe whole lot in my path. He made me angry, he made me right into a monster" I say as my fingernails dig into my palm. "You can extrade again" He says. "What if I don't need to" I say standing, fists clenched. "I recognize who you truely are Samantha, you may do this" He says putting his arms on my shoulders as I shove him off me. "You recognizenot anything Tobias" I growl out. "Come on Samantha, allow it out. Punch me, pass on I dare you" He attempts to egg me on. "Fuck off Tobias, passinterior and go away me alone" I growl going throughthe oceanas soon asgreater. "You can't do it. You recognizewe're your own circle of relativeswe adore you Samantha. You can't punch me due to the fact you care" He says in my ear as I flip and hit him withinside the face as he is going down hard. "Shit, I'm sorry" I gasp as my hand is going to my mouth in shock. "Saaammmaaannnttthhhaaaa" A voice sings withinside the distance. "Tobias, passagaininterior...NOW!" I warn as he jumps up and turns closer to the voice.

"Not a chance." He says preserving his nostril. "I heard that the large boss died today, is that authentic little one?" Greyson comes out of the darkness with Seb and Kai through his side. "Who the fuck are you?" Tobias growls. "Come domestic with us Samantha, thosehuman beings aren't your own circle of relatives, we're" Seb smiles, preserving out a hand. "Don't do it" Tobias warns. "We'll take the arenathroughhurricane Samantha, you and us" Greyson winks. "No greater Hayden telling us what to do anymore, the crowd is ours" Kai smirks. I note Tobias get out his phone, ringing a person. "Tobias, passinterior" I urge, taking walks in the front of him and taking the gun from his again pocket earlier than aiming it at him as he is taking a step again in shock. "Good girl" Seb laughs taking walks up in the back of me, kissing my shoulder as Greyson and Kai stroll up nearin the back of. Tobias walks up the stairs slowly. "The human beings we killed...They had been my guysproper?" I say turning with the gun pointing down. "Only ones that were given too near. Hayden desired you to himself, he wasn't sharing. But, we didn't need to proportion you either" Seb smirks, his finger caressing my cheek. "You drowned me **numerous** times…" I pointed to Seb. "Never **permit you to** die though" He replies. "You violated me sexually **as soon as**" I pointed to Greyson. "Your **framebecamesimply** too **suitable** to be **authentic**. I've **constantlydesired** you to myself" He winks. "You watched it all, did you **experience** it Kai?" I growled. "I watched you **experience** ripping **the onesguys** to pieces, I've watched you beat **a personinside** an inch of his **lifestyles** and take a seat **down** in his blood as your hands play with it, **with out** even realising. I've watched you **turn out to be** the **maximum** feared **girlon thisglobal** as you took down your **personal** allies **with out** knowing. But, I **additionallyrecognize** you **experiencethe fun** of a kill" His eyes sparkle. "Sam!" I **listenthe decision** of **numerous** voices coming down the stairs. "Come with us" Seb says. "He made me **right into a** monster" I **stated**. "He made you stronger" Greyson smiles. "He threatened my **own circle of relatives**" I growl. "But yet, he **in no wayharm** them **except** you made **the incorrect** move…" Kai answered. "Come with us Samantha, be our leader, take **the arenathroughhurricane**" Seb says **as soon** asgreater. "Kitten!" Jayden shouts from some metres away. "Stay away Jayden" I nameagain as he's joined through Rob, Wayne, Tobias and Lukas. "They need you to simply run the school, be a nobody, you'll be in an workplace doing office work and now no longerdwelling the lifestyles you truelyexperience. We assist you to have fun. We can take down the whole lot you hate. Killing the human beings that deserve it, baby molesters, drug runners, intercourse traffickers. We assist you to" Greyson comes toward me. "No!" Jayden shouts. "We ought to do that?" I say as I strollnear Greyson as he smirks, his hand on my chin. "Of course, however one little thing..." He says his hand on my waist. "Samantha no!" Luka shouts. "What?" I ask as I investigate Greyson's mischievous eyes. "You'll be ours and best ours, we'll proportion you, however you'll best be mine, Seb's and Kai's" He smirks. "Yours..." I closed my eyes. Why did all and sundry see me as a ownershipas though I becamesome thing that had to be owned! Something interior me snapped me out in their hypnotic keep. "Yes, be ours and best ours. You don't want them." He nodded closer to my own circle of relativesin the back of me.

"You've been looking ahead to the day Hayden misplaced me haven't you? To take me for yourself?" I ask as my hands tightened round my gun. "It became a rely of time. You could be mine" Greyson growls possessively. "There's one thing..." I stated as he tilts his head smirking. "Yes my love?" He says pecking my lips as he smirks over my shoulder. "I don't like being owned" I stated as I fired 3 times. Greyson dropped to the floor coughing up blood from the pictures to his chest as Kai and Seb drew out their personalweaponshoweverhad been shot at earlier thanthey mightgoal as they went down simply as quickly. "Say hello to Hayden for me" I snarl as I clutch Greyson through the throat and watch because themild leaves his eyes, blood pooling over my hand as my nails bit into his neck. "Let pass Sam, he's dead. Let pass" Someone pulls me off his frame as I'm dragged backwards. Something interior me snapped as soon asgreater, it became like a keep on my coronary hearthave been lifted barely as I sat shakily sobbing. "You ought to love me...You broke my nostrilSamantha" Tobias knelt in the front of me and all of sudden I became a sobbing, giggling me

Chapter Fourteen

Slowly we make our mannerinterior as my eyes take withinside the house. It became a mess, snap shotshad been strewn towards the tables, snap shots of Marcus, Seb, Greyson, Kai, Hayden and me. "How did you get those?" I ask as I undergo them, recognising while the photoshad been taken. "We had a personship them to us, we nonetheless don't recognize who" Taylor says. "Who despatched you photos of the men I becamerunning with? Why?" I ask as my eyes pass over each image. "Maybe we ought togo away this for this night and speakwithinside the morning" Rueben says as Lindsey follows in the back of him with out Cody as she had placed him to mattress. "No. Who the hell took those?" I repeat. "We don't recognize. They had beendespatched to us, we haven't had some thing else, simplyphotos, there are a fewgreater in an envelope, however we don't go away them out due to the kids" Rueben says as he opens a locked cupboard and passes over an envelope. I listenautomobiles and motorcyclesinput the driveway as I draw out the photo's from the envelope and gasp. "You realize the human beings in those?" Taylor asks. "Yeah, I'm the only who did that to all of them..." I gulp as I see the destruction I had executed over the year. "I idea you had been going to mattressyounger lady" Tobias walks in with my Grandpa in the back of him, his hands crossed as he notices the photo's in my hand. "We aren't doing this this night Samantha" Grandpa says taking the record from my arms and turning me farfar from the snap shots. "I did that..." I stated as his eyes went wide. "You had been made to. It wasn't your fault that the oneshuman beings died" He says. "Do you realize who they had been?" I ask, they had beenretainingsome thing from me. "We recognizea fewrecords yes. But now no longerthis night" He shakes his head. "They had beenharmless weren't they" I stand my floor as he turns again to me from main me from the room. "Sam, it's pleasantnow no longer to delve into this this night. We'll kind it out while you've were givena few rest" Luka enters the corridor. "Who the fuck have I killed?!" I scream as all and sundryseems at me in shock. "People we'd despatched to assistdiscover you" Luka answered. "He advised me they had beena part ofintercourse rings, traffickers, ill and twisted guys...Why did I agree with his words?" My hand went to my mouth with a puff and a sob. "Sammy..." Taylor locations a hand on my shoulder as I shake it off and run from all of them as I bolt out the again door and out onto the seaside as I scream and fall to my knees. Scenes flicker in my head of eachventure we had long gone on withinside the year. Hayden had had me kill all folks that had gotten nearlocating me, he made me kill my personal allies and I had executed so painfully. I became a killer. "Samantha..." "Leave me alone" I cried on my knees. "You aren't a monster Samantha, he did this to you, he coerced you to do this. You aren't a murderer" Tobias sits beside me. "I fucking loved it..." I appearance to him as he nods with a sigh. "You idea they had beendistinctsorts ofguys...You did what you ideabecameproper with the records you had" He says. "Nothing however a blood-soaked rose...He did it...He broke me...Turned me into what he desired...He cherished it after Igot hereagain to him blanketed in blood calling me his blood-soaked rose. But it wasn't simply me he supposed, he supposed that I became killing my personalhuman beings this complete time, I killed guys of the Midnight Rose" "You aren'tdamaged Samantha. You are higher than this. You will make it via this. It's over" He says searching into my eyes. "It's in no way over...I can't forestall this urge to needto teara person's throat out, to smashthe whole lot in my path. He made me angry, he made me right into a monster" I say as my fingernails dig into my palm. "You can extrade again" He says. "What if I don't need to" I say standing, fists clenched. "I recognize who you truely are Samantha, you may do this" He says putting his arms on my shoulders as I shove him off me. "You recognizenot anything Tobias" I growl out. "Come on Samantha, allow it out. Punch me, pass on I dare you" He attempts to egg me on. "Fuck off Tobias, passinterior and go away me alone" I growl going throughthe oceanas soon asgreater. "You can't do it. You recognizewe're your own circle of relativeswe adore you Samantha. You can't punch me due to the fact you care" He says in my ear as I flip and hit him withinside the face as he is going down hard. "Shit, I'm sorry" I gasp as my hand is going to my mouth in shock. "Saaammmaaannnttthhhaaaa" A voice sings withinside the distance. "Tobias, passagaininterior...NOW!" I warn as he jumps up and turns closer to the voice. "Not a chance." He says preserving his nostril. "I heard that the large boss died today, is that authentic little one?" Greyson comes out of the darkness with Seb and Kai through his side. "Who the fuck are you?" Tobias growls. "Come domestic with us Samantha, thosehuman beings aren't your own circle of relatives, we're" Seb smiles, preserving out a hand. "Don't do it" Tobias warns. "We'll take the arenathroughhurricane Samantha, you and us" Greyson winks. "No greater Hayden telling us what to do anymore, the crowd is ours" Kai smirks. I note Tobias get out his phone, ringing a person. "Tobias, passinterior" I urge, taking walks in the front of him and taking the gun from his again pocket earlier than aiming it at him as he is taking a step again in shock. "Good girl" Seb laughs taking walks up in the back of me, kissing my shoulder as Greyson and Kai stroll up nearin the back of. Tobias walks up the stairs slowly. "The human beings we killed...They had been my guysproper?" I say turning with the gun pointing down. "Only ones that were given too near. Hayden desired you to himself, he wasn't sharing. But, we didn't need to proportion you either" Seb smirks, his finger caressing my cheek. "You drowned me numerous times..." I pointed to Seb. "Never permit you to die though" He replies. "You violated me sexually as soon as" I pointed to Greyson. "Your framebecamesimply too suitable to be authentic. I've constantlydesired you to myself" He winks. "You watched it all, did you experience it Kai?" I growled. "I watched you experience ripping the onesguys to pieces, I've watched you beat a personinside an inch of his lifestyles and take a seat down in his blood as your hands play with it, with out even realising. I've watched you turn out to be the maximum feared girlon thisglobal as you took down your personal allies with out knowing. But, I additionallyrecognize you experiencethe fun of a kill" His eyes sparkle. "Sam!" I listenthe decision of numerous voices coming down the stairs. "Come with us" Seb says. "He made me right into a monster" I stated. "He made you stronger" Greyson smiles. "He threatened my own circle of relatives" I growl. "But yet, he in no wayharm them except you made the incorrect move…" Kai answered. "Come with us Samantha, be our leader, take the arenathroughhurricane" Seb says as soon asgreater. "Kitten!" Jayden shouts from some metres away. "Stay away Jayden" I nameagain as he's joined through Rob, Wayne, Tobias and Lukas. "They need you to simply run the school, be a nobody, you'll be in an workplace doing office work and now no longerdwelling the lifestyles you truelyexperience. We assist you to have fun. We can take down the whole lot you hate. Killing the human beings that deserve it, baby molesters, drug runners, intercourse traffickers. We assist you to" Greyson comes toward me. "No!" Jayden shouts. "We ought to do that?" I say as I strollnear Greyson as he smirks, his hand on my chin. "Of course, however one little thing..." He says his hand on my waist. "Samantha no!" Luka shouts. "What?" I ask as I investigate Greyson's mischievous eyes. "You'll be ours and best ours, we'll proportion you, however you'll best be mine, Seb's and Kai's" He smirks. "Yours..." I closed my eyes. Why did all and sundry see me as a ownershipas though I becamesome thing that had to be owned! Something interior me snapped me out in their hypnotic keep. "Yes, be ours and best ours. You don't want them." He nodded closer to my own circle of relativesin the back of me. "You've been looking ahead to the day Hayden misplaced me haven't you? To take me for yourself?" I ask as my hands tightened round my gun. "It became a rely of time. You could be mine" Greyson growls possessively. "There's one thing..." I stated as he tilts his head smirking. "Yes my love?" He says pecking my lips as he smirks over my shoulder. "I don't like being owned" I stated as I fired 3 times. Greyson dropped to the floor coughing up blood from the pictures to his chest as Kai and Seb drew out their personalweaponshoweverhad been shot at earlier thanthey mightgoal as they went down simply as quickly. "Say hello to Hayden for me" I snarl as I clutch Greyson through the throat and watch because themild leaves his eyes, blood pooling over my hand as my nails bit into his neck. "Let pass Sam, he's dead. Let pass" Someone pulls me off his frame as I'm dragged backwards. Something interior me snapped as soon asgreater, it became like a keep on my coronary hearthave been lifted barely as I sat shakily sobbing. "You ought to love me...You broke my nostril Samantha" Tobias knelt in the front of me and all of sudden I became a sobbing, giggling mess.

Chapter Fifteen

Luka lifted me from the floor as my frame shook from rage, hurt, anger, love and ache. "Tobias! Let me repair your nose" Lindsey gasped as he chuckled as my eyes darted to his with a small smirk. "There she is" He smiles as all of themhave a take a observe me with worry, however I can sense their gazes lighten on thenotion I turned into smiling. "Bed time girly" Taylor says as Lukas contains me upstairs with Taylor in tow as they plonk me with the aid of usingthe toilet so I can wash up. "I don't need to be on my own" I mumble as I stand in my pyjamas with the aid of using the mattress. "You won't be" Savannah comes into the room. "We notionit might begreat Jayden didn't are available in tonight." Savannah stated. "Does he hate me?" I ask. "Of path I don't hate you kitten" Jayden says from the doorway. "You ought to..." I appearance to the floor. "I mightin no way hate you and I will wait tillyou'regeared up, till the ends of the earth. I love you kitten" He says with a involved smile. "Thank you" I sob as Savannah takes my hand an squeezes it tight. "Goodnight kitten" Jayden says because the others depart me withinside the room as Savannah climbs into the mattresssubsequent to me. She startsbuzzing a lullaby and stroking my hair motherly as I doze offwith the aid of using her side, tears falling from our eyes. We'd ignoredeverydifferent too, she turned into my brother's wife, howevercertainly considered one among my greatpals too. "Layla! Can you snatch Samuel for me?!" A voice shouts waking me from my desires. "Yes uncle Shaun!" Layla shouts lower back with a giggle. "Who the fuck is Samuel?" I murmur as I pay attention Savannah laugh beside me. "Elise and Shaun's kid...Quite the handful for a six-month-vintage" She answers. "I...Shit...I forgot she turned into pregnant..." I murmur as she hugs me tightly. "It's adequate. It will take time to get used to matters again." She says as we climb out of the mattress. "Mummy" Cody groans wiping his eyes from the mattresswithinside thedifferentnook of the room. I had woken numerousinstanceswithinside thenight time and simply watched him. His eyes had been getting brighter like his father's and I couldn't assisthowever be mesmerised with the aid of using them. "Hi toddler boy" I stated as I picked him up as he smiled and cuddled into me. "Samuel! No!" Shaun shouts as I pay attention a crash. Savannah opens the door and we creep out the room and down the steps as we watch the hilarity spread as Layla is chasing after a crawling six-moth-vintage little boy as Louisa is walkinground1/2 ofbare. "Louisa! Why aren't you dressed?!" Savannah calls out as Louisa giggles at her mum and runs off. "So we've a loopy six-month vintage, a bare five-yr-vintage and an eleven-yr-vintage chasing the others at the same time as my -yr-vintagebaby is flawlesslysatisfied and behaving in his moms arms" I smirk as Savannah offers me a grimyappearance. "He's been recognised to reasonhassle too, simply you wait" She smirks. I stroll down the steps and controlto grab up Louisa as she runs beyond as she giggles in my arms. "No!" She screams, giggling as I byskip her over to Savannah. "Thank you" Savanah takes her and stomps up the steps to get her dressed. "I need to get down now mummy" Cody says kissing my cheek as I permit him get down. "Samuel! Come on!" Layla shouts as she struggles with the lovable little boy. "He's a achesimilar to the female he turned into named after"

Shaun grumbles as he wheels himself out of the **living room** as I **improve** a forehead as he notices me. "And who **turned into** he named after?" I ask with a smirk. "Oops..." He blushes. "You can't be serious...You **men** named him after me?" I **chuckle** as I **assist** Layla **select out** the little **man** up and **region** him on his father's lap. "Of **path** we did." He smiles "Good morning Sam, I see you've met our son Samuel" Elise comes out of the kitchen with a smile. "Cody! No! Not my hair!" I **pay attention** Layla scream as she storms out of the kitchen with banana mashed into her hair. "I **informed** you" Savannah comes down **the steps** as she laughs passing Layla who **turned intodashing** to **the toilet** to **easy** her hair. I **stroll** into the kitchen to **discover** Cody sitting with a **massive** grin on his face as he's smashing banana everywhere. "Cody" I say sternly as his grin disappears. "Mummy! Want **a few** banananananananan?" He says **preserving** out **a bit** as I **chuckle, not able** to **hold** my **immediately** face. "You **wantto mention** sorry to Layla **whilst** she comes down again. You can't **positionedmeals** in peoples hair" I urge as he frowns. "Sorry mummy" He says and **is goinglower back** to eating. "Trouble, **similar to** his mother"

Lindsey laughs kissing my head as she maintains to prepare dinner dinner eggs at the stove. "How did you sleep?" Grandpa asks as I take a seat downamong him and Cody. "On and rancid all night time. I discovered myself looking Cody, he has this have an effect on of chasing the horrificdesires away" I solution as I smile at my little boy. "Cody move RAWR at horrificdesiresand that theymove away! Daddy informed me!" Cody smiles. "That's proper little guy, we move RAWR at a horrific dream and display them we aren't terrified of them and that they run away" Jayden walks in and kisses Cody's head, smiling faintly at me, delight in his eyes at Cody. "Jay" I smile. "Come for a stroll?" He says and I nod, following him out onto the deck out the lower back as we close the door in the back of us. "I recognisethe whole thing has occurred so quick and you've been thru so much. I turned into so scared I misplaced you. But closingnight time made me recognizesome thing. Proposing to you couldnow no longerhad been the finestconcept so soon. You don't need to sense owned and I in no wayneed you to sense that with me. I in no wayneed you to sense trapped, so in case youneedto mention no to it, proper now, then it's adequate, I can wait tillmatters are higher or making a decision you don't need to be with me. I'm right here for you, always" he says in a hurrysearching down. "Jay…Look at me…This beyondyr I turned into owned with the aid of using Hayden, he caged my coronary heart, he destroyed me piece with the aid of using piece. But, simply being domestic, I'm going to get there, with all of you. I do want time, however I'm now no longer taking this ring off…Not ever…" I say as his eyes mild up with a smile. "You nonethelessneed me?" he smiles. "Of path I do. But…But…There's a part of me that's scared that while youdiscoverthe whole thing he did, You won't need me." I say as he slowly reaches for my hand however pulls it lower back as I take it slowly myself. "Don't do that. No rely what I am right here. I don't care. I love you Samantha, you're my one and only" He says as I smile and squeeze his hand. "Baby steps" I say as he squeezes lower back. "Anything for you" He smiles and leads us lower back indoors, our palms entwined collectively. "Sammy, might you thoughts coming to paintings with me these days? I simplyneed to get you a righttest-up" Lindsey says with a understanding glance. "Is some thing wrong?" Jayden frowns, his eyes searching over my frame. "She's been thrulots Jayden, matters take a toll, I simplyneed to make certainthere has been no lasting damage" Lindsey answers. "It's adequate Jay, I'll come. Better to be safe" I smile at Jayden. If I turned into pregnant with Hayden's baby I nonetheless had no concept what I might do. "I'm coming too. Doctor desires tohave a take a observe the scarring these days anyway" Taylor provides as I observe him sitting up on the bar, his palms interlinked with Damien's. "Why do I sense like there's extra to this?" Jayden asks. "Sammy will informall peoplewhilst she's geared up Jayden" Lindsey offers him a stern appearance as he sighs and nods, freeing my hand and supporting to easy Cody's face. The residenceturned into so busy of my own circle of relatives coming in and out, tryingto test on me, trying to spend time with me, that I turned intohappyto depart the residence with Taylor, Lindsey and Damien. Taylor and Damien went off to their appointment as I accompanied Lindsey into an ultrasound room. "Hello Samantha, I'm Doctor Traver, I'll be searching at you these days. Lindsey gave me a short history. Said you've been thrulotsthese days and desired a brieftest up. First, we can do an ultrasound and testthe whole thing out internally after which we'll appearance externally quick." The health practitionerstated shaking my hand as I turned intocaused the table, Lindsey taking my hand in hers. "Thank you" Is all I stated as he started his search. "So, seems like you've were givena bit scarring, have you ever been in a few fights?" He asks. "Yes" I solution. "Ok, so there might also additionallyhad been a tear and it healed, it appearsadequate, however we'll take any otherappearance in some months. Now, the womb, shall we take a glance" He says as he actions the probe down as I near my eyes. "Ah, have you ever been sexually active?" He asks. "Yes" I squeak out nervously. "Well it seems like you're pregnant" He says as my eyes dart to the displayto looka bit blob of a toddlerat thedisplay. "Shit, no, no, no" I cry as Lindsey squeezes my hand. "Excuse me for my forwardness howeverturned into this a rape case?" the health practitioner asks. "Yes, however theguy is now no longer alive, so police aren't needed" Lindsey pipes up because thehealth practitioner nods. "Although I ought torecord it, I won't this once. But please, get a fewassist. I can see the scars Samantha, there's extra to this. I'm guessing you comprehend it all Lindsey" The health practitioner sighs as she nods. "We've were given her" Lindsey answers. "Ok. But please come see me, for something Samantha in case youwant it" he says as I nod. He prints off a picturegraph of the toddlerexperiment and maintainsto test me over. "Your frameappears to berecoveryhowever I can pay attentiona bit fluid withinside the lungs so I'm going to get you a fewremedy for feasible infection. Have you had hassletogether along with your lungs these days?" He asks. "I...Yes" I solution. "I want the reality I want to recognise what this may be" "I turned into drowned, numerousinstances...By the toddlers father...It turned into punishment" I stated quietly. "Lindsey..." He says sternly, giving her a glance of annoyance. "You accept as true with him?" I ask Lindsey as she nods. "What the bloody hell goes on?" He asks as I inform him the whole thing, I permit him in on the whole thing from after Iturned intomore youthful to now as he sits there in shock.

"So, now you recognise…" I finish. "You ought to be dead…Your frame shouldn't be capable ofaddressthat quantity of stress… How…Why… From now on you return backand notice me personally, understood?" He says wiping his quit his face in shock. "I haven't anyconcept how she does it Felix, however she's robustand is deriveddomestic to us each time" Lindsey smiles. He maintainsto speak to us and communicate falls to the toddler as my coronary heart is cut up on what to do. "At the quit of the day, it's your choice. But with the aid of using the sounds of it Samantha, your baby is your lifestyles and this one will bethe whole thing to you. No rely who the daddyturned into. It's nonetheless your baby" Felix says. "I'm maintaining it…I simply don't recognise how Jayden's going to take it…We had been going to paintings on our personalchildrenearlier than this occurred…We knew it might behard for me to have any otherbecause itturned into and now I'm pregnant with the aid of using Hayden…" I stammer as a tear falls. "Jayden loves Cody as his personal…He'll love this babysimply as much" Lindsey says with a smile. "Yeah…He's a superb dad" I say with a smile, he surelyturned into a superb dad and he cherished Cody with all his coronary heart. It wouldn't be smooth with this little one, howeverperhapswe might make it paintings too. "Well thanks Felix, Taylor and Damien simply messaged me that they're done. So they'll take you domestic." Lindsey stands. "Samantha, take my card. If you wantsomething, name me" Doctor Traver, Felix, offers me his card as I smile with a nod. "Thank you, I will" I smile as we depart the office. "I suppose he's taken a liking to you" Lindsey laughs wiggling her eyebrows. "He's vintagesufficient to be my dad! Plus, I actually have Jayden" I chuckle. "Yes, Jayden's been so good. But, he turned into terrified the day you went missing. Savannah took over searching after Cody for some time as Jayden scoured for you for weeks earlier than he sooner or latergot heredomesticwhilst Tobias ordered him lower back. Your Grandpa and Tobias gave him a stern speakme to and he targeted on Cody, he have becomethe daddy Cody needed. They eachhad been torn with the aid of using your disappearance and constructedeverydifferentlower back up." Lindsey says as we strollcloser to the entrance. "I'm so fortunate to have him" I sniffle. "You're fortunate to have everydifferent. Finding love, isn't smooth, however the love you have, it's for lifestyles. Hold directly to it. Don't permit this beyondyrpreserve you lower back" She places a hand on my cheek and palms me the toddler ultrasound picturegraph. "Do you surelysuppose he'll be adequate with this?" I ask searchingon thepicturegraph. "He'd do something for you. You should be honest. You shouldgrow to beyour self again. One step at a time" She smiles as she friendsround my shoulder and I flipto look Taylor and Damien heading out of the hospital. "What's that?" Damien factors to the picturegraph. "Oh shit...You surely are pregnant..." Taylor gasps. "What?!" Damien exclaims. "You didn't inform him?" I ask Taylor. "Not for me to inform Sammy" He shakes his head. "Tell him" I say as he is taking Damien's hand and veers him off to a bench to provide an explanation forthe whole thing as we wait. Damien's eyes flicker over to me as he runs over and hugs me to him. "You went thru all that?" He whimpers. "Yeah...But I'm domestic" I cry. "How many others recognisethe overall story?"

He asks **freeing** me from his grip as he cuddles into Taylor's side. "You, Taylor, Lindsey, Rueben, Tobias and Grandpa" I **solution**. "Jayden doesn't **recognise?**" He **appears** at me wide-eyed. "I'm going **to inform** him **these days**...All of them **these days**..." I say, biting my lip with nerves. "Wait **till** tonight. I'll **collectall peopleand** get them **domesticcollectively**. We'll **try thiscollectively**. You're **now no longeron my own** in this" Lindsey says as I nod. Taylor, Damien and I **determined** on going for a **pressurecollectively** to **assist** calm my nerves as we rode our motorbikes round. I **observedsome thingacquainted** as I signalled for them to **comply with** as we stopped **close** to a **massive** building. "What is it?" Damien asked, **disposing of** his helmet. "That's **wherein** I **turned into kept**" I answered. "What? You **had been** so **near** us this **complete** time!" Taylor shouts. I get off the **motormotorcycle** and head **closer to** the building.

Chapter Sixteen

"Sam! Don't do somethingsilly!" Taylor shouts as I close to the constructing, the door turned into1/2 of open as I driven it, it swung to expose the corridors empty. "I'm calling Tobias, simply wait till they get right here first earlier than you move in" Taylor says protecting my arm. I carry my hands to my lips and whistle because it echoes via the halleven as Taylor holds me beside him. "There's no personright here Taylor" I shake my arm from his grip and head internal. "Sam!" Damien shouts as they eachobserve me in. Papers have been strewn throughout the floor, rooms have been empty, now no longer a weapon or individual in sight. "Taylor! Sam!" Tobias booms from the entrance as he and some of his guystyphoon in. "Up right here!" Taylor shouts as they make their manner to us. "I advised you to liveplaced!" Tobias booms. "Sam went going for walks in. Did you need me to go away her on her very own?" Taylor snapped lower back. I stepped in the front of a couple of doorways I knew all too well. "What's in there?" Damien asks as Rueben steps at the back of us and passes a gun to Damien. I attemptcommencing the door and it doesn't budge. "Look"

Taylor factors to the floor as blood is seeping underneath. "Out of the manner" Rueben warns as he and Tobias kick down the door. The phrases traitor have been written throughout the wall in blood as a frame hung from the ceiling, soaking wet in blood. "Oh shit..." I murmur. "Who is it?" Damien asks as I step ahead, my palms being lined in blood as I pull the frame down. "It's Marcus" I answer. "Who couldtry this? You killed Seb, Greyson and Kai, who else should have achieved this, this need towereachievednowadays, the bloods too fresh" Rueben exams his frame. "Did everybody ever locate Craig?" I ask. "No...You don't assume he did this? Do you?" Taylor asks. "He turned intorunning for Hayden, he knew wherein I lived earlier than, he might have beenthe only who did the photo's too" I stated. "He's now no longercleversufficient, nor sturdysufficientto thread up Marcus like this" Damien says as I stand listening tosome thing, a quiet bang. I strollamong the men as I head down the hall cautiously. "Sammy? Where are you going?" Tobias calls out as I flowsimilarly down the hall. "Shh!" I name out, finger to my lips as I pay attention a noise once more. The simplest room left turned into the room I'd been tortured in earlier than as I kicked it open. "Oh shit" The individual shouted as I walked into the room. "Looking for me?" I smirk at the person cowering withinside thenook, he turned into bruised and bleeding, Marcus had glaringlyharm him badly earlier than dying. "You killed them all! He turned into a traitor! I killed Marcus due to the fact he betrayed Hayden!" He shouted. "Who did you locate sweetheart?" Tobias comes into the room. "Craig" I smirk. "We'll take him in and cope with him" Tobias stated as I wheel round to him in anger. "He's now no longer leaving this constructing alive Tobias" I growl. "Don't depart me to her! Tobias! I swear I'll do something! Don't depart me together along with her!" Craig cries out scared. "You killed Marcus, you attempted to harm my own circle of relatives" I shout as I strollas much as him as he crouches withinside thenook afraid for his existence. "I gave them the photo's I proved to them you have beennonetheless alive!" He shakes. "Not for his or her benefit...For Hayden's, the greater they knew I turned into alive the greaterhuman beings they despatched out... I tore guysasidedue to the fact you helped Hayden...You aren't making it out

166

alive **nowadays** Craig" I snarl as I **grasp** his hair and drag him to the **center** of the room. "Samantha I will **now no longer** stand **right here** and watch you kill **some** otherindividual!" Tobias booms. "Then get out" I order as I kick Craig **toughwithinside the** face as he lays **at theground** shaking. "Sammy no, you're **higher** than this" Taylor says from **the** entrance. "Am I?" I **respond** as I pummel into Craig's face as he screams in pain. "Please! Don't kill me!" He cries, peeing himself from fear. Which **simply** spurred me on, smirking. "Samantha Jones come **right hereproper** now!" My eyes dart to **the entrance** as my Grandpa **appears** at me angrily from **the entrance**. "Sorry Grandpa, **however** no" I shake my head as my **handspress** slowly into Craig's eyes as he screams in pain, they pop **towards** my **handsbecause** the blood spurts everywhere. Once **once more** I'm **included** in warm, sticky blood as I stand, Craig screaming **at thefloor**, his **palms** over his face, bleeding to **demise** in **pain** as I smirk. "Nothing **however** a blood-soaked rose" I **sniggeron thecountry** of me as I push **beyondevery** person as they stare in shock. "What the hell **turned into** that Samantha?!" Taylor grabs my arm and twirls me round. "THAT turned into revenge, THAT turned into for killing Marcus and THAT will take place to everybody who comes after me or my own circle of relatives!" I shout angrily. "You've were given to permit this move it's ingesting you up Sam." Taylor takes my chin in his palms. "When I realize that each son of a complain that turned intoconcerned with Hayden is useless, then I will permit this move" I shake freed from his grip. "It will by no meansgive up Sam, it by no means does! Let it move!" Taylor grabs me once more as I glare at him. "Get your palms off of me Taylor" "No, I'm now no longer going to look at you ruinyour self over this! Come domestic and live with us, don't do some thingsilly like going after them" Taylor begs. "blood soaked rose, blood soaked rose" I mumble to myself final my eyes. "STOP IT! You aren'ta few blood soaked rose! That's Hayden going into your head. You are Samantha Jones, badass female of the Midnight Rose, mom to a lovely little boy who desireshis mom, you're our own circle of relatives, we want you Sammy" Taylor sobs as I investigate his eyes. "I'm sorry, I'm so sorry Taylor" I sob as he's taking me in his fingers tightly. "It's adequate Sammy, I've were given you babe" He says stroking my hair as I destroy down. "We need to get going" Tobias says at the back of him quietly as I destroy from Taylor's grip. "Tobias, I'm sorry" I say as he smiles at me earlier than kissing my head. "You've been viaplenty little one, I don't blame you for looking to kill him, I simply didn't need you to have to." He sighs. "He's now no longeruseless" Grandpa says at the back of him as they drag Craig out, a jacket hung on his eyes. "Let him bleed to demise, he merits it" I say. "Tobias, we located the CCTV unit, we've were given all photos we shouldlocate" One of the men comes out protecting a toughpressure. "Give me the pressure, take him to the cells, wrap him up" Tobias orders. "Let him die" I snap as he appears at me. "We maywantfacts from him as of but Sam" He sighs. "Information, he's a fucking weed, he doesn't realizesomething! I can't accept as true with you need to permit him stay!" "Sam, come on, we want to get you lower backdomestic" Taylor takes my hand. "Give me the pressure" I order protecting my hand out. "Why?" Grandpa asks. "Because I needto peer what's on it myself earlier than you lot watch it and in all likelihood see me doing matters I by no meansneed you to peer!" I shout as realisation hits their faces. "Fine" Grandpa nods because thepressure is given to me, I placed it in my jacket pocket as I get on my bike. "HE will die" I factor to Craig who'snonetheless crying out approximately his eyes in pain. "When we've had a bit chat, yes" Tobias sighs and nods. I nod and placed my helmet on as I begin up my bike, Taylor and Damien race to observe as I head domestic. "Sam, you're included in blood, don't be sillywith the aid of using storming internal!" Taylor shouts as we park up. I shrug and head into the house, fortuitously it's quiet as I head upstairs. "Daddy! Play airplanes with me!" I pay attention Cody's voice laugh as I pay attention Jayden making aircraft noises. I smile as I peek in to the bed room as I see Jayden swinging Cody round playfully. Suddenly I'm dragged away right into a bathroom. "What the fuck is inaccurate with you?! What if Cody noticed the blood on you? What passed off?!" Savannah exclaims at me. "I...Fuck...I don't realize...We...We located the region that I turned intosaved in and...Marcus is useless, Craig killed him...Savannah, I'm dropping my mind, I overwhelmed Craig's eyes with my nakedpalms and loved it" I cry as she appears at me in shock. "Craig meritsthe whole thing he gets. You have to speak to us, inform us what's happeningfor your head babe, we willsimplestassist if we realizethe whole thing" Savannah kisses my head earlier thanassisting me easy up the blood. I open my jacket as I take out the toughpressure and the infanttest as I lay it down at theaspect as she is going wide-eyed. "What...Are you...Oh babe" She sighs caressing my cheek softly. "It's going to kill Jayden I even have Hayden's babyinternal me" I cry. "Jayden loves you he won't care, he simplyneeds you to be secure, glad and he loves Cody, he'll love this infant too. This infantmay have a loving own circle of relatives and an superb daddy in Jayden. But you need to be sincere with him" She says searchingon theinfanttestbecause the finger grazes over the photograph with a grin. "I'm telling every personthis night what passed off, all of it" I mention. "Good, however what's that?" She nods to the toughpressure. "One of Tobias's guyslocated the CCTV from the warehouse...I don't **realize** how **an awful lot** is on it **but**...I'm scared to **appearance**" My hand shakes **choosing** it up. "We can **appearance** together" Savannah **locations** a hand on mine. "No, I won't **have you** ever watch it, **now no longer** after **the whole thing** I've **achieved**" I shake my head. "Someone **need to** be with you Sam you can't **try this** alone" "Sammy? You in there?" I **pay attention** Taylor **name** out. "We're **each** in **right here** Taylor" Savannah calls out as she opens the door. "We're **looking** that with you, no excuses" Damien says **at the back of** Taylor, pointing to the **toughpressure**. "No, I won't **have you ever** watch me be the monster I **turned into**" I shake my head. "Sam, that **turned into** all Hayden **owning** you, you **aren't** that **individual**. Let us **assist** you" Damien says. "Ok..." I murmur. "Sammy? Guys? I didn't **realize** you **have beendomestic**" Jayden comes out of the bed room frowning. "MUMMY!" Cody runs **as much as** me as I **select out** him up, kissing his cheek. "Hi **infant**" I smile as he nuzzles my neck. "Me and daddy **have been** being air planes!" He giggles. "I **realizeinfant**, I **shouldpay** attention you giggling, did **you've got got** fun?" I ask. "Yeah! But now I hungry" He frowns as his belly gurgles. "Well how approximatelyyou return back with me and we'll make a few lunch for every person buddy, mummy and daddy wantto speak" Savannah says as Cody jumps from my fingers to hers with a laugh as she offers me a understandingappearance, the testwith the aid of using my hand nonetheless as I nod. "We'll come up withmen a minute" Taylor smiles, kissing my head as he's taking Damien's hand and heads downstairs. "What's happening?" Jayden asks, taking my hand softly in his as my eyes near at this touch. "I...Ok, I'm going to simplypop out with it...I'm pregnant, it's Hayden's, he tore me aside mentally and bodily he claimed me, made me right into a monster and I'm so scared Jayden. I recognizein case youneednot anything to do with this infant or me due tothe whole thing that passed off. But simply promise me you won't depart Cody I shouldcope with it with time, however that little boy dotes upon you" I cry as I can't undergo to study him as I move silent. "You assume I couldabandon you...Look at me Samantha" He tilts my head up with a finger as my eyes meet his, tears clouding each our eyes. "You are my internationalinfant I couldn't staywith out you and it kills me to assumeyou watched I could abandon you or Cody. I turned into so scared to lose you and now I have you everlower back I by no meansneed to lose sight of you once more. I usuallydesired a largeown circle of relatives this infant will simplyupload to it. No remember the father, we are able toincrease it together. You are my existence Samantha and you'll be my wife. We will cope withthe whole thing together, simply don't depart me kitten, by no meansdepart me" He says as I cry and fall into his fingers as he hugs me tight to him. "I love you Jayden" I murmur in his fingers as he holds me tighter, kissing my head. "I love you too infant, a lot" He says. As we launcheverydifferent I wipe my eyes as his eyes locate the test and the toughpressure. "Is that the infant?" He asks choosing the test up. "Yeah" I nod. "The toughpressure...What's on it?" He frowns as he wipes of a blood fingerprint from it. I give an explanation for what had passed off and what will be on it as he sighs, a hand going over his face. "I'm looking it with you" He says finally. "No you're now no longer" I say as I grab it from the aspect and stroll out. "Samantha, permit me watch it with you, permit me be there for you" He says as I typhoon off. "No, you don't wantto look at this, are you telling me you'llneedto peerthe whole thing Hayden did to me?!" I cry out. "Yes! I needto peer what passed off to recognize what my female went via so I can assist her" He thunders lower back. "You needto peer him drown me! Taser me, rape me! You needto peer him lick blood off my frame as he were given off on it, due to the fact that's what he did, whenever I killed a person he ordered me in his room, licked the blood from my frame as he raped me. Is that what you actually needto peer?!" I shout. "Hayden did what?!" A voice exclaims as I turn. "Zane...You of everybodyneed torealize what that guyturned into like" I murmur. "I by no meansnotion he'd...We need to have were given to you quicker, I need to have long gonelower back to him, however they wouldn't permit me! I turned into going to headbelow cover, Tobias wouldn't fucking permit me. I should have were given you out!" Zane swears. "No, you wouldn't have achieved. Hayden could have killed you instant Zane." I sigh. "I'm looking the photos with you Sam, whether or notyou want it or now no longer" Jayden says as he plucks it from my palms and wanders off down the steps as I groan and observe. "What's happening?" Tobias says as he and my grandpa are stood chatting. "Watching this fucking thing" Jayden lifts the toughpressure up as he is going into the study. "Give that to me moron, you crashed the laptopremaining time you have been on it" Damien says as he's taking it from him and starts offevolvedrunningat thetoughpressure. "I assume I'm gonna be sick" I groan with nerves. "We're properright here" Zane places a hand on my shoulder as I see Tobias, Jayden, Damien, Taylor, Grandpa all nod. "That's what I don't like" I sigh as Damien placesnumerousdisplays of photos up straight away as we study his 3displays. One turned into of my bed room, the second one Hayden's workplace, 0.33turned into of the hallway after which the very last ones confirmedevery cell. "How an awful lotphotos is there?" I ask as I see the date of the photosturned into recent. "At least a years-worth" Damien mumbles. "Great" I sigh as he's taking it to the start and places it on speedyahead. "There's wherein they added Sammy in" Taylor says as I see them dragging me into the celled room. My palmsstarted out to shake as we watch on, the torture of that week starts offevolved as I right here them seethe, looking as I'm harmwith the aid of using the guys. "I don't experience so awfulapproximately Marcus anymore" Taylor grumbles. Then they ahead it to after Iturned into first included in blood as Hayden took me in his fingers, licking the blood from my frame as he raped me time and again. "Please prevent" I cry. Fast ahead to torturing guy after guy as they screamed. One after some other as they watched the displays, their faces displaya variety of emotions. "Please prevent, I'm a monster" I cry. "You're now no longer a monster Sam" Jayden says as I lose it, I take the laptop from Damien as I carry up a surefactor, the worst kill, the person I tore aside as Hayden laughed manically. "Oh yeah, how approximately now?" I say as they watch in horror. "That turned intodue to Hayden, Sam, that wasn't you" Tobias gulped. "Sure seems like me" I snap as I flick viaa number of the worst instances as they watch on. Then we get to the region being empty, Marcus coming into on his very ownearlier than he's accompaniedwith the aid of using Craig and some otherguy.

"I knew he couldn't do it on his **very own**" Taylor murmurs as we watch carefully. "Who is that?" I ask as Damien enlarges it. "Callum Hanst" Zane **solutions** with a frown. "You **realize** him?" Tobias asks. "He's young, impressionable, does as he's **advised**, **absolute confidenceturned intorunning** with Craig **due to the fact** he had nowhere else **to head**" Zane frowns. "Great **simply** what we **want**. So **wherein** did he **move?**" Grandpa grumbles as Damien watches him **via** the **photos.** "He didn't **depart...**" Damien says as he watches him dart **right into a** vent **withinside theidentical** room as Craig. Craig smirks as he shoots him **withinside the vent and pushes his framesimilarly** in. "Well, he's **now no longer** an issue..." Zane murmurs. "He **turned intoproper** there **withinside the** vent, **useless** and we **by no means** noticed..." Taylor murmurs. "We'll get **the child** out and **deliver** him a burial" Tobias sighs. "Will you **permit** me **end** Craig **but?**" I ask. "No, he's **useless already**" Tobias **solutions.** "WHAT?!" I exclaim. "He bled out **earlier than** we **were given** him to the basement" Tobias says. "Shame" I **statedparadoxically** with a smirk. "Can we **speakapproximately** the elephant **withinside the** room **for a** minute...Hayden, what he did..." Jayden sighs. "What's to speakapproximately? He did it, he fucked with my head and impregnated me. End of story" I say. "YOU'RE PREGNANT?!" Zane exclaims. I be aware Damien going viacomponents of the photosonce more. "Damien prevent it" I snap. "It's now no longer you Sam, this wasn't you, you wouldn't try this" Damien says flicking via the photos. "It WAS me Damien, each fucking bit, he made me tear human beingsaside, appearance, LOOK! That is ME!" I pause it as I'm smirking up on thedigital digicamincluded in blood, simplyearlier than Hayden took me to his workplace. "Mummy..." We whirl round as I see Cody wide-eyed searchingon thedisplay screen as I rush as much as him and take him out the room. "Why have been you all included in blood at thedisplay screen?" He murmurs, sniffing like he turned intoapproximately to cry. "Mummy...Mummy..." I stammer. "Mummy turned intoassistinga person that turned intoharm. You don't want to fear little guy" Jayden says kissing his head. "Not mummy's blood?" He sniffs. "No, appearance I'm all secure, no boo boos" I smile as he appears at me. "Good, don't like mummy harm" Cody hugs me tight as I wrap my fingersround him. "Jayden make certain that photos is scrapped" I order as he sighs and nods. "Mummy come have lunch, Aunt Sav and me make sand...sand...sand witches" Cody wrinkles his nostril as I laughon the cuteness. "You suggest sandwiches, now no longer sand witches, except there's a magic witch inflicting a sand typhoon!" I gasp dramatically. "NO! Don't be stupid mummy, we make sand witches, with ham and cheese" he grins as I snigger. "Ok, permit's moveconsumea few sand witches" I laugh as he's taking my hand and leads me into the kitchen. I pay attention the menpop out of the workplace as I attempt todeliver them a small reassuring smile which they return. "The toughpressure is locked up for now" Tobias says as I'm sat on the counter with Cody. I glare at him. "We wantto test who else turned into in there, make certainno person comes after you" Damien says as I sigh and nod. "Daddy, have a sand witch!" Cody shouts as he palms Jayden a 1/2 of of his sandwich. "Yum" He grins stuffing the whole lot in, making Cody laugh. "Such a pig" I shake my head with a grin as Jayden makes pig noises which reasons Cody to snigger louder as I watch them happily. "You're **now no longer** a monster, **that** is who you are. You are a **momtogether** along with **herown** circle of relatives who has **achievedmatters** to survive. We love you **irrespective of** what" Grandpa says in my ear as a tear drops down my cheek. "MUMMY! Mummy no cry!" Cody sees it as he wiggles out of his chair and leaps into my **fingers** as I **warfare** to **trap** him. "Cody, don't **soar** like that!" I say sternly as he pouts. "Sorry mummy don't like mummy crying" he hugs me tight. "I'm **gladinfant, now no longer** sad. I **simply** love you **a lot** and **neglected** you." I kiss his buttery cheek with a **laugh**. "Mummy no **departonce more**" He says planting a **big** slobbery kiss on my cheek. "Never" I smile as he giggles. "Hey Cody, how **couldyou want** to be a **large** brother?" Jayden smiles. "What **suggestlarge** brother?" Cody frowns. "That you had a brother or sister, if mummy had some **otherinfant**?" Savannah smiles at him. "Mummy having a **infant**?!" Cody **is going** wide-eyed. "Yes infant boy" I nod. "Baby brother?" He asks. "I don't **realizebutinfant**, it is **probably** brother or a sister" I chuckle. "I don't **need** sister, **women** icky" Cody pouts. Jayden laughs. "Girls are **first rate** icky" Jayden laughs. "HEY! I'm a **female**" I shove him playfully. "No, you mummy, **now no longerfemale**" Cody laughs. "Yeah **stupid** mummy" Taylor sniggers. For the **relaxation** of the day we **simply** spend time together, Cody clinging to me **all of the** time as he spoke to my **belly, speaking** to the brother he **desired** as **all of us** giggled at him. I felt like a load had come off my shoulders as I **turned intocapable ofexperienceregular** for once. By the **nightevery personturned intodomestic, however** I had **advised** Tobias I couldn't **preserve** telling **human beingstime and againonce more** what had **passed off,** so he did it for me, he took them into the **workplace** and **definedthe whole thingtillevery** person knew. I **turned intopositive** he **confirmeda number of** the **photos** as a **fewgot here** out **lightconfrontedsearching** at me **earlier than** hugging me tight. Even Abraham Henderson **got here** over as I hugged him tight to me, he **turned into** sticking **round** for **a biteven as** too and had promised **to speakviamatters** with me as he used to in school, **nearly** like a counsellor. My **entireown** circle of **relativesturned intoright here** and **despite the fact that** I felt like a monster, none of them **checked** out me like that, they have been scared that I coulddestroy, they desired to preserveassisting me lower back up, preserve me glad and get via it. I turned intodomestic, secure with my own circle of relatives.

Chapter Seventeen - Epilogue

When you've got gota lot to do in lifestyles time flies with the aid of using and an entire12 months had flown with the aid of using from after I had escaped Hayden's clutches. Our most recent addition Melissa become the noisiest toddler I had ever known, in comparison to Cody. Cody have been so quiet and now Melissa screamed the residence down all of the time. The handiestcharacter she stopped for become me, she couldcontinuously cry for me, so I ended up doing the whole thingtogether along with her strapped to my chest. Cody could get jealous from time to time and throw a tantrum simply to get interest and I attempted to do my fineto present him simply as a good dealinterest, however it wasn't usuallyclean. He ended up in Jayden and I's mattressmaximumnight time claiming he had nightmares, however I knew it becomesimply to get near me as Jayden attempted to cope with Melissa everynight time. Jayden had trulycome to bethe daddy they each needed, he dealt with them like his very own and cherished them dearly. Luka absolutely took over The Midnight Rose for me as I went thru this pregnancy, it wasn't an clean one. I had struggled and ended up in health facilitynumerousinstances on a drip. We'd all been scared that I could lose the toddler, however we saved going and become so gladwhile she in the end arrived. I had no plans to movereturned to mafia lifestyles, I becomecentered on own circle of relatives and the college. After speakme to Henderson we notionit might befine if I took a backseat for some time to get my head returned to regular and he becomeproper. I becometaking part injogging the college, the childrenhave beenextraordinary. We have been pushing an increasing number of that childrenkeep away from this type oflifestyles, looking todeliver them the capabilities to stay a regular and gladlifestyles. Most appeared to take it on board, howevera few horrors have been too deeply engrained in a few as while the graduated they went directlyreturned to the gangs they used to know. But we may want torelaxationcleanunderstanding we did our fine and gave them the capabilities they needed. Taylor and Damien had followed a candy little boy known as Tommy who have becomefinepals with Cody nearly immediately, you mayslightly separate them after theyhave beencollectively. They have become an exquisiteown circle of relatives unit themselves as they sold a small cabin close by to stay in. Luka, Savannah, and Louisa determined to liveon theresidence as Luka becomeusually so busy with the Midnight Rose and Savannah and I have beenusuallypreservingeverydifferent company, she become my fine friend…Apart from Taylor. James and Rob have beenneverthelesssingle, however they appeared to experience it, relationshiplots of quitegirls as they hung out in bars and clubs. James appeared to experience being uncle greater than some thing and took the function seriously, he cherished the children. Tammy and Wayne had their fingerscomplete with Rosie the canine and Layla who becometurning into a stroppy teenager, I attempted to preservean eye fixed on her as she wandered the halls at college, however she appeared to take after me in boarding college, usuallyinflictinghassle. But maximum of the time she listened to me as I instructed her off for her behaviour, she desired to be robust like me. She becomesimply going the incorrectmannerapproximately it, so I helped her, she began out to get better, however she becomeneverthelessa touch rebellious, I mean...what youngsterager isn't? Shaun, Elise, and Samuel have been doing extraordinary too. Shaun had truly taken to coachingat the same time as in his wheelchair, he cherished racing approximately in it and by no meanspermit it get him down, he embraced the whole thing. Including supporting me get returned to topbodilyenergy, teasing me that I wasn't brief enough, despite the fact that I becomejoggingsubsequent to him in his chair. Every day I remembered the ones we had lost, and every12 months we had a campfire to install a message to our cherished ones as we as soon as did at the beach, it have becomeculture that unfoldin the course of the campus too. Tobias, Rueben, and the biker membership all saved themselves busy withinside thecollege as they travelled a ways and huge to acquirechildren that have been in hassle to carry them to us. Grandpa retired in the endat the same time as Lindsey determined she desireda pairgreater years as a nurse earlier than she would go away the health facility. She stated she may want toby no meanssurrender her activity so after she couldcome to be a element time nurse for the college which we agreed to, the childrencherished her. Grandpa and her, spent a lot time on thecollege as childrendealt with them with a lotappreciate, it become heart-warming. Life becomesearching up and I becomeglad. "Sam you ready? Wow" Taylor smiles at me brightly as he seems over my body. "I experience sick" I murmur as I appearance down on thestunningwedding ceremonyget dressed I become wearing, the bodice become corseted with white lace masking it right all the way down to the fishtail backside which dragged over the ground. "You appearancestunning girl, Jayden's going to explode" Taylor winks as I snort. "That's the closingissue I wantproper now, I'm neverthelessgetting better from the closingtoddler" I snort. "Oh you realize you'll have every other with him" Taylor smirks. "I'm quitepositive he desires topaintings on it tonight" I snort nervously. "You'll grow to be with an army" Taylor laughs. "And we'll love eachone in every of them" I smile. "Time to take to the aisle sweetheart" Grandpa walks in as I wolf whistle, he **seemsgood-looking** in his suit. "Daaaaammmnnn Grandpa" I smile as **he's taking** my arm. "See you up there Sammy" Taylor winks as **he's taking** Layla and Cody up the aisle **earlier than** us, my hand shakes with my rose bouquet. "Deep breathes, **that isthe personyou likeentire** heartedly, **neglect aboutall** people else, **simply** you and Jayden" Grandpa squeezes my hand. "Thank you Grandpa, for **the whole thing.** I love you" I smile as he hugs me tight **earlier than** we **stroll** to the door. "I love you too, now **permit's get you hitched"** He smiles because **thedoorways** open **to expose** me the aisle as **all people** stands **both** side. I **pay attentionsome** gasps as we **strollbeyond** them, **however** my eyes are on him, he hasn't **seemed** up **but** as Cody is tugging on his leg excitedly as I **snort.** "That **youngster"** I sigh **fortuitously** as Grandpa chuckles. "MUMMY!" Cody turns and sees me **because the** crowd laughs. Jayden **in the endseems** up and all I see is adoration in his eyes as he **seems** at me, I smile brightly. "You **appearancestunning"** Jayden murmurs as **he's taking** my fingers from Grandpa. "Not too **terribleyour selfgood-looking"** I wink. I take a **briefgo searching** me at my **pals,** my own circle of relatives and surprisesimply how we were given to this point. Today I become marrying the person who fell for me after all of the torment and hassle I have beenthru. He have been there thru thick and thin. He become my international and have becomethe daddy my kids needed. "Ladies and gents we come right herenowadays to unite youngerfanatics in holy matrimony, Samantha Louisa Jones and Jayden Christopher Bennet. We'll begin with Jayden, please repeat after me" He says as he says the traces for him to repeat. "I Jayden Christopher Bennet promise to present you the fine of myself, to accept as true with and appreciate you, to proportion with you my time and interest and to carry joy, energy and creativeness to the connection we have. I will love you for all eternity." Jayden says as he seems into my eyes. "I'm bored" Cody whispers to Taylor as all of ussnort. "Shh toddler boy, be carried out soon" I whisper as he huffs. "Sorry" I blush. "No problem, now Samantha, repeat after me" The priest smiles brightly. "I Samantha Louisa Jones promise to present you the fine of myself, to accept as true with and appreciate you, to proportion with you my time and interest and to carry joy, energy and creativeness to the connection we have. I will love you for all eternity" I grin as he squeezes my hand as a tear escapes my eyes. "So, exceptevery body has rumour as to why thosehuman beingscan not be wed..." He says pausing as I pay attention Cody huff once more as I boost a forehead at him with a smirk, a finger to my lips because the others chuckle. "Troublemaker like his mother" I pay attentionGrandpa murmur as I snort. "Then it's far my electricity to claim you each husband and wife, you can now kiss the bride" He smiles because the crowd cheers. "Oh I will" Jayden smirks as he's taking my lips passionately. "YUCK!" Cody gags. "Cody!" Taylor laughs chucking him over his shoulder as he giggles. "That youngsterwill becomean increasing number ofsuch as youevery day" I snort to Jayden. "Funny, clever and witty?" Jayden smiles as human beings take photos. "A entireache in my ass" I wink earlier than he acts stunned and sweeps me off my ft with a chuckle. "You simply married me, regretting it already?" He smiles. "Never" I grin as he kisses me. The crowd cheer as Jayden contains me away as all of us head to the college for the reception. "I love you Mr Bennet" I smile. "I love you too Mrs Bennet" He twirls me and kisses me passionately as soon asgreater. This becomeone of thefine days in my lifestyles and I couldn't await our future. One collectivelyfor all time with our children, runningon thecollege and preservingall of thechildrensecureon thisloopyinternationalbecause the legacy of The Midnight Rose travelled a ways and huge. Spreading energy, love, and own circle of relatives bonds as a manner to stayon this harsh international. Family, we won't have all of itcollectively, howevercollectivelywe'd have all of it. With a touchenergy and love we may want to have some thing we desired.